Quite simply, we were so beautifully matched—our needs so perfectly meshed—that our experience that afternoon was much more glorious than it had any right to be. Even what might have been drawbacks turned into advantages: His shyness made him cautious and gentle, and my inexperience made me, in a curious sense, adventurous. Once, for example, after he had tickled my nipples into tingling erectness, I reciprocated by putting my mouth to his and gently sucked first one then the other while he, astonished, tried (but not very hard) to stop me. I didn't know that men weren't supposed to find their nipples a turn-on and, indeed, I had William twisting with pleasure.

Different parts of the body have vogues, I've noticed, and it's only been recently that men have allowed themselves pleasure through their nipples. On that autumn day in 1967, at sixteen, in a Yale dormitory, I did a little trailblazing out of sheer ignorance.

Diane

A True History by Herself

A DELL/EMERALD BOOK

Published by
Emerald Books
8/10 West 36 Street
New York, New York 10018

ISBN: 0-440-01736-X

Printed in the United States of America

First printing—August 1982

Chapter 1

You can hear anything in New York. I had left my downtown studio—the one I call the "other" studio; the one hardly anyone knows about—and stepped out into the swirl of Thirty-third Street. It was barely past noon, and I was late, so I headed toward Sixth Avenue to grab a taxi. Trucks and cars jammed the street, and their drivers, with nowhere to go, pressed horns and screamed at each other. The walks were just as congested, but there was motion: salesmen hurrying with their sample cases, wearing polyester suits and frowns; white-aproned boys delivering delicatessen sandwiches to harassed dress manufacturers behind scaly facades; a tall black strolling with a sheaf of fox pelts thrown over his shoulder; and, coming from all directions, racks of dresses, raincoats and blouses, careening through the human wall like padded torpedoes.

A black-haired, hungry-eyed Puerto Rican with a blaring transistor radio perched on his shoulder pushed a rack of swaying identical blue dresses beside me and said, "Babee, I wanna eat your mango."

Like any woman who's been in New York for

more than five minutes, I knew the only reaction was to look straight ahead and keep walking, pretending I hadn't heard. But I wasn't like any woman, particularly after that morning. So I laughed, looked down at him and said, "If I had the time you *could* eat my mango, and I'd throw in a couple of papayas for nothing."

His eyes popped and his face lit up as his mouth dropped open. He'd had a vision of the promised land.

"Babee, I got the time, I got the time," he said, hurrying to keep up with me. He was frantic not to lose what must have seemed the most unobtainable woman on the street: a tall, blonde, long-legged, smooth-skinned, brown-eyed beauty. I'm not conceited—I'm still so insecure I keep checking my reflection in store windows—but I know how I appear to men and I knew how I looked to him. For the past four years it's been my business to know.

I reached Sixth Avenue, hailed a cab and jumped in as he rushed to the curb. Gaily, good-naturedly, I waved good-bye as the cab pulled away, leaving him with his radio and dresses and frustration.

Then I felt mean. I shouldn't have teased him, I thought. I had spent the morning being teased, and I hadn't like it, even though I'd been paid for it. With a sigh, I gathered my portfolio and equipment bag on the seat beside me and gave the driver—one of those kids who obviously was hacking while on the way to something else—the address of my uptown studio, the respectable one.

As we darted through the midtown traffic, I

rummaged in my case to make sure I had everything I'd need that afternoon. From among the film, lenses, light meter and cameras I pulled out one of the test Polaroids I'd made that morning. There he was, in color, wearing nothing but sunglasses. I wondered what the driver would think if he knew his respectable, professional, classy passenger was studying a picture of a man with his cock and balls dangling along his thigh.

Then I wondered what I thought of the same woman. I'd become so accustomed to depersonalizing myself—to seeing myself as others saw me—that I hardly paid any attention anymore to my own feelings and judgments. Here I was, rushing from the garment district to a Central Park West penthouse studio. I was going to complete an assignment that would help establish my name as a fashion photographer, and at the same time I had rolls of film that were decidedly unfashionable tucked away in my case. I was the center of three careers, each beginning to flourish, and I wasn't willing to give any of them up. I would have to make a choice—one of these days. But not right away.

I looked at the picture again, and then reached into the bag for another. He stood, arms akimbo, legs apart, still wearing the sunglasses, defying the camera. I smiled as I remembered the look on his face when he had arrived at the studio that morning.

"Is D. Bourne here?" he asked, looking around the loft. He was, I guessed, about my age (I later learned he was twenty-eight, two years younger than me). And he was tall. Since I'm five foot ten, and have always been self-conscious of my height, any man who is taller than I am is automatically attractive, even if he looks like Quasimodo.

This one was no Quasimodo. He was perfectly proportioned, standing in his black boots, with tight jeans and a checked shirt open almost to the waist. His hair was light brown, as were his mustache and the curling hair on his chest. He wore mirrored aviator sunglasses, the sort you can see yourself in. Slung over one shoulder was a canvas backpack. He stood tentatively at the door, looking into the bar loft.

"I'm Diane Bourne," I said, giving him a cool, professional smile.

"Oh, you're a woman!" He didn't move, and I was afraid he was going to leave.

"That's right," I said crisply, stepping around him to close the door. "Come in and put down your things. You can change behind that screen." I pointed toward the other end of the room.

"I'm here for *Playtime,*" he said dubiously, naming the magazine I was to do the layout for, as though he wasn't sure I understood.

"That's right. You're Randy Wrong."

"Well, yeah . . . that's my professional name."

"OK, Randy," I said, all business, "just step over and get out of those clothes and we'll get right to work."

Still he hesitated. I understood why. The loft is bare, with only a couch, a few panels and lights along one wall. It looks abandoned.

And even I was not reassuring, because I didn't look like any photographer he'd ever seen before. I made a point of dressing as though I were going to lunch at La Grenouille when I worked at that studio. Some perverse streak in me insisted that I wear my best. On that day I was in a Diane von Furstenberg shirtdress, bright pink, and had four Elsa Peretti gold chains around my neck. My hair had been done the day before by Harry King, and fell to my shoulders in a blonde mass. On my ears were two simple gold clips. I was out of place in that loft, on that street, in that profession. No wonder he was thrown off. I liked it that way.

I continued smiling and raised my eyebrows slightly as I pointed again to the screen. Finally, he walked behind it with determination, like a man who has accepted the inevitable.

While he was undressing, I spread a paisley bedspread over the couch, turned on the lights and positioned the reflectors. Then I got my cameras out of the case and loaded them.

From behind the screen he asked, "How do you want me?"

"Let's begin with nothing on at all," I said briskly.

He stepped from behind the screen, stark naked. I watched him openly as he walked to the couch; whether he was looking at me or not I couldn't tell because he had kept on his mirrored sunglasses, which rendered him expressionless.

"OK, Randy," I said, "stand by the couch while I do a couple of Polaroids to check the lights and position."

He stood, his legs apart, his hand at his waist, and pointed those reflecting eyes at me like some monster insect. He had been born with a good body, and had helped it along with weights; each muscle in his shoulder and arms was defined, and his pectorals, capped by hair-surrounded nipples, billowed from his chest. His stomach was a series of ridges—lines so sharp they might have been etched. His cock was uncut and thick, and hung a quarter of the way down to his thigh; framing it was the biggest scrotum I'd ever seen, encasing two huge balls in its hairy membrane. The legs were sturdy, with muscled thighs and bulging calves. He was quite a hunk.

I focused and clicked, and waited the minute for the picture to develop. The silence was charged, so I put on a punk rock tape—but softly. I took the picture out of the camera and saw I had to adjust the lights.

"Is this your first appearance in *Playtime*?" I asked in a chitchatty voice, as though I were discussing nasturtiums at a suburban gardening club. I moved the lights into place.

"Yeah." He remained as he had stood, with feet apart, cock dangling.

"I'll do another test shot." I clicked and waited again. Still he stood unmoving. I wished he'd take off his sunglasses, but I didn't want to risk making him hostile—and hence uncooperative—at this stage, so I said nothing. The developed picture showed everything was fine, and we were ready to begin.

"OK, Randy," I said seriously, "let's start with some sideway views—some tease shots." As soon as I had seen him I decided to do a series that would keep his cock out of full view until the reader turned to the centerfold, and then would open it to find all of him. The editor who had commissioned the series—a woman I knew only over the telephone—had given me carte blanche. Though a large part of the audience was gay men, *Playtime* was ostensibly a sex magazine for women, so at least half its staff were women, and all were feminist, which is one reason I got the assignment. Most of their beefcake was shot by men, simply because I was one of the very few women in that line of work.

The punk tape was thumping like a diseased heart as I smiled graciously and said, "Now, what I'd like to do, Randy, is begin with a few shots of you standing with your leg forward like this," I showed him with my own leg what I wanted; I didn't touch him, "in order to keep your cock out of camera. Shall we begin?"

He turned dutifully, and woodenly thrust out his leg. The pose was miserable, but I shot a few anyway to loosen him up. "You know," I said, "I think I'd like to try it without the sunglasses."

It was impossible to see his expression, but I felt him stiffen. "Uh . . . the sunglasses are my trademark," he said.

"Well, then," I said brightly, "this'll be a breakthrough for you, won't it?" My smile was steely and firm.

Still he hesitated. "I like to keep them on."

"I think you'd be better without them." I wondered whether he had some defect—maybe his eyes were crossed. Even so, I was determined to give the readers of *Playtime* every centimeter of Randy Wrong.

Still he hesitated, and still I stood adamant. Finally I wore him down with my stare; reluctantly he removed the glasses and handed them to me. His eyes were large and, surprisingly, blue-grey—a little like a Siberian husky's. And, even more startling, they were shy. With his glasses, Randy Wrong was a sex machine; without them, he lost his menace, but gained a whole new dimension of appealing vulnerability. I had admired Randy's pecs and shoulders, his thighs and legs, his ass—like two globes—and his back which formed a perfect Vee; I had marveled at his cock and balls; but it was when I saw his eyes that I began to feel moist between the legs.

He was sulky, as though I had been an overly strict camp counselor. I was excited, not only by him, but by the greater possibilities of the layout, now that I'd glimpsed this quality in him. I rushed ahead. "Let's try the side shot again, Randy," I said. "Look at me now over the shoulder. Lower the head a little. That's right." Click. "A little lower now, Randy." Click. "Give me a little lip, a pout." Click. "Open the eyes, Randy." Click. "Wider. Keep them sexy, Randy." Click. "Give us an invitation, Randy." Click. "Tense the biceps—attaboy. . . ."

He was getting into it, and so was I. His body became relaxed, more fluid and languid. The muscles gleamed as he sweated under the lights. I kept coaxing, urging, caressing with the camera, and he became looser and voluptuous. "Open the mouth a little, Randy." Click. "A little more, baby, like you're having trouble breathing." Click. "Give us some tongue now. Along the upper lip." Click. "Ohhh, that's hot, Randy. Narrow the eyes and keep the tongue out, baby." Click. "Hump a little. Keep those eyes on me. Keep the leg out, baby." Click. "Cup your tit, baby—cover with your hand." Click.

"OK. Now turn a little more toward me. A three-quarter view." I hoped to find an erection, something to correspond to my own increasing heat. But his cock hung huge and flexible, and stayed that way as I talked him through another series of shots.

"Lie down on the couch now, Randy," I said, reloading the camera. "Let's begin with you lying on your stomach, and see what we come up with." I sounded businesslike and crisp, but there was a mist of sweat over my forehead, and the Chanel I was wearing was rising musky and strong to my nostrils. He was sweating too, but he was under the lights. He stretched out on the couch, and turned those pale eyes to me with a question.

"Ummm," I said, casually, "that's right. For starts. Now spread the legs a little and put your hands over your head . . . grab the cover—bunch it up. That's right." Click. "Look at me, and pull your left leg up." Click. I did a series on his ass, with just a hint of balls showing beneath it.

"Turn over, Randy," I said, reloading my camera, "and lie on your back. Spread your legs." Click. "Run your hand down your thigh. That's right. Now cup your balls." Click. "Good, Randy. Now wet the lips and narrow the eyes and look at me, baby. Gimme an invitation. That's right." Click. "Pull your left leg up and stretch your right leg out. Spread 'em. That's right. Spread 'em wider." Click.

I crouched and leaned to get my shots, and

then pulled over a high stool and sat on it with my own legs spread and my skirt above my knees, as though I were careless. I wasn't careless, though. I wanted him to see my crotch and get ideas.

"Keep your legs open, Randy, and play with your balls. Push your cock up on your stomach. That's it." Click. "Keep your hand there, now, and look right at me. Wet your lips." Click. "Open your mouth, baby, show some tongue, narrow the eyes." Click. "Give more sex, Randy. Make it hot." Click. "Squeeze the tits—make 'em stand up with your arms. Attaboy. Now look right at me and play with your cock." Click.

I was hot. My pussy was so wet I thought it must be dripping through my panties. Randy was responding to the camera with all the right motions; the shots I was getting were going to be terrific. But I wanted him to respond to me, too; I wanted him to get a hard-on for me. He didn't. His cock was as flaccid as when he walked through the door.

I got off the stool to reload the camera. "OK," I said, "we'll do another series. I'm going to need an erection." I looked at him, I hoped not coyly, and asked, "Think you can manage that?" It was a stupid thing for me to do. I know how sensitive men are about getting it up; I've seen the wrong words turn the most aggressive stud into jello. The worst thing you can do to some men, I knew, was to challenge them in that area; I suspected that Randy, with his pale blue-grey, vulnerable eyes, fell into that category. I had to recognize that one of the reasons I had thrown this dare at him was out of pique at his failure to acknowledge me. I was angry at myself for being so unprofessional. Contritely, I turned back to him after I had loaded the camera.

He lay on his back, gently rubbing his cock. His eyes were fixed on it, engrossed. He was breathing shallowly through his mouth, as his fingers stroked and squeezed.

I watched him, and held my breath. He licked his hand with great swipes of his tongue in order to make his cock glistening slick, then massage and coax it into tumescence. I hovered over him like a helicopter waiting for a signal to land.

The signal never came. If only he had given me a flicker of interest—shown by even a darting glance that he was aware of me—I would have been down on him like a shot. But he was self-sufficient. Maddeningly, his very aloofness enhanced his desirability; that he was so relentlessly moving toward fulfillment without any outside help frustrated me so much I trembled.

The cock was hard, thrusting out of his hairy groin like an obelisk. He continued to play with the base, teasing and caressing it; he was mesmerized.

I cleared my throat and said, "Great! Terrific! Now hold it!" To my own ears I sounded foolish, as though I were commending a Boy Scout for tying knots. My voice had a high, hysterical quality. Quickly I focused my camera and clicked. "Keep holding it up and look at me, Randy." Click. "With both hands, now, frame the cock and balls." Click. As I again took charge of the session, my voice calmed down, and my trembling came under control. "Arch your back, Randy, and stick out your tits. And keep that cock standing straight up." Click.

"Good. Now do the same thing but look straight at me." Click. He continued to play with his cock, stroking it from the base upward, like someone reassuring a restless animal. He did everything but croon to it.

As I recognized that he was not going to allow me to enter his fantasy, I calmed down; I have never been one to indulge hopeless passions. I continued to bob up and down, crouching to get every conceivable angle, and finished the roll of film with a flourish. "Spread your legs wider. Now pump! I want you to shoot, Randy. Work on that cock!" He increased his rhythm and moaned. His eyes rolled back and his head twisted to the left. He was as taut as a bow just before the arrow is released. With a gasp he shot sperm into the air; straight up, and down it came, white and globular on his belly. Click. Click. Click.

"That's great Randy," I was primly congratulatory as I tossed him a towel. "We got a lot of good shots. You've been a good model." I was also just a mite condescending; another form of revenge for having been excluded.

"Uh . . . thanks," he said, still winded. He lay on his back a few moments, one leg dangling off the couch, his arm thrown over his eyes. Then he gathered strength and asked, "You got the time?"

"Twelve noon."

With a sigh he sat up. "I gotta rush," he said, looking around. "What'd you do with my sunglasses?"

I handed them to him and he put them on. He stood and stretched and gave his head a little shake, then smiled at me. Without those glasses the smile, I knew, would have been shy and friendly; with them, it was mechanical, merely civil.

He was dressed in five minutes. I was still packing my workbag when he emerged from behind the screen. He held out his hand and shook mine as he said, "Well, thanks. Uh . . . I got a show to do at one, so I got to get going."

"A show?"

"Yeah. At the Epicure."

"What's that?"

He shrugged. "A movie house, with live shows sometimes. Today it's me."

"A gay house?"

He shrugged again, as if he'd never noticed. "I suppose. Mostly."

"What do you do?"

"I jack off," he said matter-of-factly. He was at the door, and turned as he added, "That's all I ever do. I just jack off."

"Well, I hope I didn't ruin the afternoon for the Epicure's clients. I mean, by making you deposit your load here on my couch." I was being bitchy; I still couldn't forgive him for being self-sufficient when I was in the room, so hot and willing.

If he noticed my tone, he didn't let on. "Nah," he said politely. "I can do four, five shows a day. No sweat. I just jack off. To music."

With a jaunty wave of his hand he was out the door, leaving me wondering what kind of music. I was both tense and exhausted. I would have liked to masturbate, there on the couch where Randy had just shot off, but I didn't have time, since I was supposed to be at my uptown studio at noon. So I finished throwing my stuff in the workbag and went rushing down the stairs to Thirty-third Street and that invitation to have my mango eaten. God knows, the mango was ripe.

The cab pulled to the curb, and I paid the sum on the meter directly into the driver's hands. I had gotten one of the few cabs left in Manhattan that didn't have one of those scratched plastic shields protecting the operator from the passenger, or vice versa. The kid who was driving looked like the trusting sort who could have used a little protection. I thought, idly, that he'd probably have his head bashed in before the day was out.

"Excuse me," he said in an accent that was non-New York—either from the Midwest or California, or someplace like that—"but haven't I seen you somewhere? In the movies?" It was not a line, but a sincere question, politely, shyly posed. He appeared genuinely impressed.

It was one of those moments that, frankly, I live for. "You might have caught my commercial on TV," I said with a modest, self-deprecating smile. I had perfected humility; it was a mask I could snap into place, yet it was mostly real.

"Say! That's right! You're the Bin-Bin Bead Girl!"

I smiled and nodded, democratic royalty in the presence of an admiring peasant.

"That's a terrific commercial. Are you an actress?" Then, without giving me a chance to answer, he added shyly, "I'm an actor."

"Oh, that's great," I said, getting out of the

cab, dragging my gear after me. "Well, good luck."

"Good luck to you! What's your name?"

"Diane." First name only. How much more accessible could you get?

We waved and smiled at each other and he drove off, looking pleased. I felt a glow, and at the same time, felt rather shoddy. It was to encourage such occurrences that I usually dressed to be recognized in the streets. These encounters meant a lot to me, more than I liked to admit. Other models would show up for an assignment wearing faded jeans, no make-up, and with their hair still damp, but I usually tried to dress to the nines (not always possible for early morning calls). My ego needed it. Even now, as I was breaking into new facets of the business—stepping out of the lights and behind a camera—I still needed the lift that a doorman or a garment center worker could give me, by admiring my looks, or recognizing me from the ads. I knew such gratification was shallow, but I was too unsure of myself to forgo it. A cab driver, by recognizing me, could make me soar; it almost made up for having been ignored all morning by Randy Wrong.

Someday, I thought, as I headed into the building, I'm going to grow out of this need for constant reassurance. Then, as the doorman smiled and held the door, I also thought, but it won't be right away.

Chapter 2

It's not so hard to figure out why my ego needs constant massaging. I've never even had to go to a shrink for the answer. Quite simply, I grew up knowing I was ugly. This was not just an inferiority complex I'm talking about, but a rock-bottom certainty, because by all the criteria that applied to looks during my early adolescence, I really *was* ugly. I was, in fact, almost a freak. By the time I was twelve years old, I was already five foot eight, and had developed breasts so large that a bra was imperative. As if that weren't enough, I had braces on my teeth and wore corrective glasses. The only indignity spared me was acne—how I missed it I'll never know. Oversight, probably.

Children are the cruelest species around, of course, and they're particularly vile to one of their own when they sense weakness. I had almost no armor against them when I started to school, and my peers made me miserable right up to the day when I finally transformed myself, with some delayed help from nature, into a beauty.

Parents are usually held accountable for the pre-pubescent suffering of their children, but I think that's unfair—at least in my case. My parents were neither cruel nor indifferent. But neither were they very helpful. Sometimes, in looking back, I think it might have been because they simply didn't know what to do with the funny-looking child fate had dealt them. Actually, I suppose they were just wrapped up in themselves and didn't notice my misery. I was not given to tantrums or sulking or long depressions, so they didn't have much to go on. Later, when I was in high school, all the other girls were dating the boys they had grown up with, while I started dating college boys. Both Mother and Father became concerned, and we had long talks about "goals" and "appearances" and "ambitions." By then, though, we were more like polite boarders in some middle-class hotel than a family. We really didn't have too much emotional involvement with each other.

My father was a self-made man who had never had the chance to go to college, and always regretted it. In spite of what he considered to be his drawback, he started a broom factory in the small town in Connecticut where he had been born, and prospered. My mother came to the town to teach in the high school, and they married eighteen months after her arrival. She gave up teaching—without a murmur, I suspect—and settled into being a housewife. Almost exactly a year after their marriage, I was born, their only child.

Both of my parents were tall, and reasonably attractive people. They were calm, comfortable and quiet, had a few friends—other couples like themselves—and as Father's business grew, they joined a country club and Mother became more active in charity organizations. They still live almost the same way they always have: dinner at the club two or three nights a week, friends over for bridge, some TV, Mother's Wednesday afternoons with the Grey Ladies, Father's Saturday afternoon golf. . . . They're content.

I was anything but. I can't remember too much about my first few years—there were no traumas or melodramas—but as soon as I started school, life became painful. I was skinny and tall, taller than both girls and boys. I was called "Beanpole," "Giraffe," "Birdlegs"—names that seem harmless enough now, but then, when I was eight, nine, ten years old, when I only wanted to be exactly like every other child—they were cruel, as they were meant to be. I didn't fight, and I didn't ingratiate. I withdrew into myself. Soon I had developed aloofness as armor, and though the name-calling didn't stop and the pain didn't lessen, a crust of pride hid my suffering from others. Towering and ungainly, braces and glasses glinting, I would run the gamut of the school corridors, books cradled in my bony arms, nose in the air.

Then my breasts grew. I tried to disguise them—at first with loose blouses, and then by walking with my shoulders hunched forward, as though I had a heavy pack on my back. Surreptitiously I looked at the other girls. They were as flat as boards, as are most ten and eleven-year-olds, and as we grew older, none of them ever approached the full-blown dimension that I achieved.

I was thirteen when I discovered the fashion

magazines, with their pictures of sleek, perfect women. My main refuge during my adolescence was reading. I would devour anything—books, papers, magazines—and I spent hours going through the racks at the book and card shop in our town. It was run by a tolerant couple who didn't bother me once they realized I was not there to shoplift. Also, I nearly always bought something. Before long I had gravitated to the section that displayed *Vogue, Mademoiselle, Elle, Harper's Bazaar,* and all their imitations. I pored over the pages of women who were as skinny as I (though none of them had my breasts) and who stared into the camera with sulky eyes and glossy, pouting lips. I would take the magazines home, and in my locked room I spent hours in front of the mirror, twisting myself into the poses I found on page after slick page.

At fourteen the braces came off, and the glasses, having done their duty, were retired. But I still towered over the heads of my classmates, still had my upper amplitude. Though I was pretty, with honey-colored hair, large brown eyes and smooth, unblemished skin, I didn't really know it, for there was no one to tell me so, and break that spell of ugliness which had encapsulated my childhood.

Boys started noticing me, but that didn't help, because they were intimidated by my height and breasts. Their nicknames for me became less innocent: I still grow red with shame when I remember how one boy in my class, trying to impress the others, said as I passed, "There goes old Jugs." The snickers and giggles that followed cut through me like razors. But I didn't let them see my hurt; on the contrary, I started walking tall, shoulders thrown back, head still high, with an expression of cultivated indifference on my face. I practiced imperviousness, and became as haughty as those improbable creatures staring at the world from ads for fingernail polish and haute couture.

My parents were worried because I didn't have friends. My mother, in a tactful, gentle and uncomprehending way, once said, "You should be a little more friendly, Diane, and not act so snooty. I think you put others off by seeming so stuck-up."

"I don't care," I said.

"But wouldn't you like to have more friends? Go out with the other kids sometimes?"

"No." I was lying, of course. I wanted desperately to belong to a clique, to go to football games, to be asked to spend the night at others' houses.

I started high school with the hope of breaking out of my social cocoon, but after a week I realized the next four years would be more of the same. There were, it was true, a few boys now who were as tall as I (I had reached my full height of five foot ten) but I remained the tallest girl in the school, and the most developed. I was still different; by this time I found it impossible to let my guard down for an instant, and I propelled myself from class to class like a Rolls Royce that had inexplicably found itself on the Ford assembly line.

A couple of times I noticed boys getting up their nerve to talk to me, but I didn't know how to encourage them, to let them know I would be receptive to their invitations. I thought that boys had all the initiative, and that girls simply said yes or no.

The boys were, of course, shy, and as afraid of rejection as I was: when they came up against my shield of glacial indifference they cowered and backed away. I watched them disappear with a mixture of scorn and sadness. "I'm just like Brunhilde, surrounded by flames," I said to myself as one of those stalwarts slunk off after losing his boldness. "It takes a very brave guy to get near me." I had just discovered Wagner and, as was my habit, was translating my loneliness into his brand of fantasy. I tried to pretend that I enjoyed my inaccessibility, but I was confused and hurt. I could not see that the barrier I had built to protect myself from cruelty was so impregnable that it also kept out kindness.

Then I met William. I suppose it was inevitable that something or someone come along and shock me into a new pattern—and that is what William did. I was in a bookstore, at the end of the summer of my sixteenth year, just after my family and I had returned from a month at our beach house. That was the summer that I discovered John O'Hara, and decided he was the greatest American writer who ever lived. I was always making such discoveries, and plunging into some writer's universe, compulsively turning my life over to a new authority's vision.

I remember that day very well: I was tanned and wearing a white miniskirt and a pink halter top. I had just chosen two O'Hara books—*Butterfield 8* and *Pal Joey*—and had stopped at the rack of magazines to pick up *Vogue,* when I became aware of someone looking at me. Instinctively, I stiffened and made my expression forbiddingly haughty. Out of the corner of my eye, I could see I was being scrutinized by a tall male, young, unknown to me, or at least unrecognized. I was wary, but at the same time curious. I knew everyone in that town, and this was a new presence. Coldly, I looked directly at him, making sure that not one spark of friendliness or encouragement seeped into my eyes.

He was tall, over six feet, and his brown eyes were enormous, peering out of a mass of long brown straight hair and mustache and beard. Though he was dressed in that classless uniform of the mid-sixties—Levis and blue workman's shirt with sleeves rolled to the elbows—he had a privileged and educated stamp. What impressed me more than anything else was that he was an older man, probably twenty-one or two. And he was looking at me with such naked admiration—it almost seemed his mouth was hanging open—that I was flattered into holding his gaze.

"Hi," he said.

"Hello." I smiled, cool and inscrutable, though my stomach felt hollow.

"I haven't seen you before. You new here?"

"Hardly," I said, falling into my self-protective superiority. "I was raised here," I added more gently, trying not to scare this one away.

He laughed nervously. "That was a dumb question. *I'm* new here." He was, I realized, shy, intimidated by me.

"Oh?" We stood staring at each other as I, with a sinking feeling, waited for him to shuffle embarrassingly out of my life, the way the others did.

He didn't retreat, though. "My folks just

moved here, and I'm visiting them before going back to school." He volunteered the information in a rushed voice, as though he were afraid that if he didn't keep talking I would disappear.

"Really?" I smiled again. I wanted to be encouraging and friendly. I didn't know how.

"Yeah. I go to Yale. This is my last year. Prelaw, then I'll probably have to go into the army—or maybe not. I haven't decided yet. Oh, well . . . Where do you go?" In spite of his nervousness he had moved closer and I could smell the faint scent of spicy soap, incongruous with his proletarian getup.

His question unnerved me. I knew he was asking what college I went to. I didn't want to answer that I was still in high school, yet I knew I could never get away with lying. So I smiled mysteriously, the way the girls in *Vogue* smiled at the camera, when they deigned to smile.

"Gee," he said, "I'm sorry to be so nosy. I guess . . . I . . . well, frankly, I'm so surprised to meet someone like you here. I've been here over a month and I didn't realize. . . ." He blushed. "I'm rattling on, aren't I?"

"We've been on vacation," I said, "and just got back."

"We?" He was crestfallen. His large eyes showed pain.

"My father and mother and me."

"Oh, that's great!" He was so delighted he laughed, and I noticed that his teeth, gleaming out of his beard, were even. His breath was clean and sweet. "My name is William," he said, holding out his hand. "William Allen."

"I'm Diane Bourne," I took his hand. It was hard and firm, and encased mine. We stood for a moment, hand in hand. I could not become accustomed to his shyness, and the fact that, apparently, I was in command of the situation. I would have liked to put him at ease, but I was too tense myself to help anyone else. The difference was that I had learned to disguise my uneasiness, and he had not. As we stood, holding hands, all I could think was that as soon as he found out I was only sixteen, and wasn't in college, he'd leave. I didn't want that to happen.

"Look," he said in a rush, "I'd really like to see you. Maybe we can go to a film tonight? That is, if you're free?"

I hesitated, just long enough to create a cloud on his expression, before I said, "Yes. That'd be nice." I had not answered immediately because I didn't know how I'd manage to see him without letting him learn all about me. I was so certain that if he knew who I really was—a sixteen-year-old high school student who had no friends—he'd lose interest in me. But I decided I would take the risk.

"That's great," he said, with a broad smile. "Where do you live?"

Again I hesitated. Then, offhandedly, thinking fast, I said, "Oh, I'll just meet you at the theater."

He was nonplused, but pleased that I'd accepted.

We saw each other almost every day for the next two weeks before he returned to Yale for the fall semester. Of course, he finally met my parents, and he did learn that I was only sixteen, but by that time I had so impressed him with my facade that he seemed to think my age beside the point.

My parents, however, were not as taken in as he, and they did not approve of my going out with someone so much older than myself.

"He's a perfectly fine boy," said my father judiciously, "and his father is the new vice president out at AMCO. They've joined the club. But. . . ."

"But, dear," added my mother, "shouldn't you be seeing boys your own age?"

They had never understood that boys my own age didn't know what to make of me. I didn't try to explain. Instead I grew sulky and adamant, and finally, though with much reservation, they gave in.

"It's only going to be for another few days," my mother said, with a sigh, "and then he'll be going back to school."

"To Yale," added my father wistfully.

The idea that William would be leaving so soon was difficult for me to deal with. Our two weeks were probably among the most joyful—and at the same time the most nerve-racking—I've ever experienced. On the one hand I was seeing and being seen with a tall, handsome, older man, and on the other, I was constantly afraid I would do something that would betray the insecurity that was at the core of my personality.

William was incredibly sweet. I can understand why he was intrigued by me: I was a beautiful girl, though I didn't know it, and my personality was a mixture of innocence and sophistication. I looked older than my sixteen years, but not in any garish or tasteless way. In fact, today, looking at those ten, eleven and twelve-year-old models who can be packaged in such a way as to appear ageless, I think I must have been a precursor of that breed. William always treated me with exaggerated respect, holding doors for me, making sure I liked our tables at the restaurants we went to, solicitously taking my arm as we crossed a street. I had never been so cosseted, and I adored him.

On our last date before he left for Yale, we drove around and finally parked by a little lake on the edge of town and talked. There was a spark of expectation between us as well as sadness, as we both sat staring straight ahead at the calm surface of the water.

"Diane," he said after a silence, "I'm really going to miss you." He took my hand.

"I'm sorry you're leaving," I said. It was probably the most sincere remark I had allowed myself to make to him.

He leaned over and kissed me, a chaste kiss, with barely the tip of his tongue brushing my lips, but like his other kisses, it made blood gallop through my veins.

"We don't have to stop seeing each other," he said, still holding me. "You'll come up to Yale for a weekend, won't you? Maybe for a football game. And I'll be home for holidays."

I didn't answer, but just held him. He caressed me, again chastely, touching my cheeks, my arms, barely brushing my breasts. I made no move, either to encourage or demur. I didn't know what was expected of me, and was more frightened of being gauche than of anything else. Finally, he started the car, drove me home, and we kissed good night and good-bye.

He called two weeks later to ask me to Yale for a football game and a party afterward. My mother immediately said no, and my father backed her up, though he was not so vehement; he was impressed by Yale.

I was determined to go, and would have gone even if they had tried to lock me in my room, which they never would have done. There were several days of arguments, silent meals, exasperated and sorrowful looks, and finally they came around: I could go, but there'd be absolutely no question of my staying for a weekend. I could leave Saturday morning and come back Saturday night.

"But the party is Saturday night," I said.

"Now listen, young lady," said my mother at her most severe, "we're already going against our better judgment by letting you spend even one day with a boy who's too old for you. If you can't come back Saturday night—no later than midnight—then you just can't go. Now that's that."

I recognized the finality in her tone, and grumpily agreed. I see now that my poor parents had a terrible dilemma on their hands. Their daughter, whom they loved, was finally becoming more social, which is what they'd been urging for years, but in a much too grown-up way. On the one hand, they could hardly prevent me from seeing William, but on the other, it would be too much to ask them to be happy about it.

So I went to Yale. I drove down in Mother's car, alone, wearing a tweed miniskirt, pink cashmere sweater and, as a final touch, pearls. I felt mature and worldly. I arrived at William's dorm, where he was waiting with several other boys, all wearing Levis and tee shirts. They grew respectfully quiet as I got out and waved and William, I could see, was proud. He came rushing down the walk, kissed me quickly and said, "The game's in a couple of hours. Would you like to freshen up a bit and then look around?"

"Sure," I replied.

He led me past his friends, who nodded and smiled, into the dorm—one of the older buildings near the center of the campus—and up to his room. "We just went co-ed a little while ago," he said. "Would you believe that there was a time when a man couldn't have a girl in his room?"

"Isn't that silly," I said.

We both laughed nervously as we entered his room. It was barely big enough for a single bed, desk and chair, a reading chair and a chest of drawers. Through its two windows, the tops of trees—still green—swayed in the warm September sun. Beyond the rustle of their leaves there was little sound as he closed the door and we stood, awkwardly, in the small space.

"Well," he said, "I'm sure glad you could make it."

"So am I."

"Uh . . . would you like to stretch out a bit?" He indicated the bed.

"Yeah," I said without hesitation, "that'd be

nice." I kicked off my shoes and primly lay on my back, my arms by my sides, hands folded over my stomach. I smiled at him. "Why don't you rest too? For the game." It seems incredible that I was so innocent, but I was. I had no idea what a girl visiting a boy's dorm was supposed to do, so I followed the first suggestion William made. What's more, I doubt whether seduction was uppermost in his mind when he made his invitation—both to come to the game and to stretch out. I'm sure he had thought about fucking me, but I doubt he really believed there was much chance of it. With all the vaunted sexual liberation of the mid-sixties, there were still areas of reserve and inexperience to be found. William and I comprised one of those little pockets at the beginning of that afternoon.

"Well," he said with a nervous laugh, "yeah, I guess so." He hesitated, then unlaced and kicked off his boots and joined me, lying on his side, his head propped on his hand, looking at me.

I looked back for a long while. He touched my face with the tips of his fingers, tracing a line from my temple to my lips so lightly it felt like being dusted by butterfly wings.

"You're very beautiful, Diane."

I took his hand, kissed it, and led it to my belly. He leaned over and kissed me on the lips—a gentle, barely moist brush of skin. I held his head, my fingers playing with his thick long hair. With a sigh, he moved his face to the hollow of my throat and his tongue caressed my neck. I pulled his head closer, and pressed against him, as his hand moved from my belly, tentatively, toward my breasts. He blew lightly into my ear, then stuck the tip of his tongue in it, causing me to gasp. He was creating sensations in me that I had never realized existed, and I had no formula for responding to them. His hand cupped my breast as his thumb grazed, rapidly back and forth, the nipple, which had become so tender I shivered.

I drew my left leg up in a crook, and covered his hips with it, pressing my crotch to his. Through the layers of pantyhose, tweed and cotton, I could feel the stiffness of his cock, constrained against his leg. I was both eager and fearful. This was not a book; this was really happening.

We lay on our sides, and William's hand followed the contour of my body from my breast to my ass and then, delicately, it moved under the short skirt to my thigh. He groaned, and his mouth covered mine; his tongue swelled between my teeth and met my own. Our two tongues prodded each other as our saliva mingled and our breathing became abbreviated.

I pulled him closer, my hand on his waist. I would have liked to feel his ass, but I didn't dare: I was constrained, afraid of doing the wrong thing. Our mouths still joined, William rolled over on top of me, and wedged his knees between my legs. I felt open and accepting; though I was fearful, I had decided that this was going to lead to "it." And what's more, I decided, that was exactly what I wanted, whatever "it" turned out to be.

Raising himself on his elbows, William looked down at me. His face was flushed and his eyes were both questioning and determined; he breathed rapidly through parted lips, and his chest heaved. I moved my hands beneath his white tee shirt to his bare back, and ran my fingers up his spine, feeling the vertebrae like little pebbles in a neat row. He raised himself to his knees and quickly pulled the shirt over his head and tossed it on the floor. His chest and shoulders were broad and tanned, and a narrow line of brown curly hair ran from his navel up his abdomen, and spread around his nipples. Holding my eyes with his, as though trying to spot the least glint of resistance, he delicately took the edge of my sweater and pulled it up to my breasts. He lowered his mouth to my navel and, rapidly flicking his tongue over my skin, he covered my belly with lapping little kisses, each of which made my muscles contract in exquisite apprehension.

I writhed under his tongue as I held his head with both hands, alternately pulling him toward me and holding him back. When he reached my breasts he blew on them, then pulled my sweater over my head. He gingerly unsnapped my bra and, without completely removing it, buried his face in my cleavage while he licked first one then the other half-bared breast. With his kisses he nudged the bra aside and exposed my nipples. I trembled as the cloth grazed them, and gasped as he gently took one between his teeth.

I thrust upward, my belly against his, our sweat mingling. Neither of us spoke. We watched each other, gauging our reactions with our eyes. He removed the bra, pulling the straps along my arms, and dropped it to the floor on the growing pile of clothes. Then he stood by the bed, one hand stroking my hair while, with the other, he unbuttoned his Levis and stepped out of them. His cock strained against the white cotton briefs, distorting his crotch with its long rigid imprint. I put my hand on his inner thigh, just below his underwear. With a sharp intake of breath he closed his legs, capturing my hand in a firm, hairy, gentle grip. After running his hand from the crown of my head, down my neck, across my breast and along my belly, he searched my skirt for the catch, and found it. I raised my hips to allow him to pull it down, leaving me wearing only pink pantyhose and my very proper pearls.

He knelt over me, his ass on my knees, and began to roll down the top of the pantyhose; he would uncover an inch or so of skin and then caress it with his tongue. I trembled as he grew nearer my pussy, waiting for the touch of his tongue. William never did actually go down on me, however; not that I was disappointed. Instead of pressing his lips to my pussy, he licked around it—the belly, the inner thighs. He pulled the pantyhose off my feet and stood again by the bed, poised over me; then swiftly he peeled out of his briefs and his cock sprang from his belly, taut and quivering, pointing straight ahead.

His cock, I now know, was about average size—six or so inches—but it was the first I'd ever seen, and it looked huge. The head was red and there was a bead of clear liquid shimmering on the tip. William leaned over and, with his mouth on one of my nipples, carefully inserted a finger in my pussy, working it back and forth, gently manipulating, caressing the labia with his thumb. My thighs felt flooded; I was both tense and eager, wanting his cock, but afraid of it.

He kept his finger in my pussy as he opened the top drawer of the bureau near the bed, and took out a small square packet. With his teeth he ripped the covering, then pulled out the pale, rolled membrane within. He fitted it over his cock, and rolled it up the shaft until the edge was lost in the denseness of his pubic hair. The cock, now sheathed, rather like a statue before unveiling, still fascinated me; I don't like rubbers now, but then anything he did would have been exciting.

He removed his finger from my pussy and looked at me, seeming to go over every inch with his eyes. My legs were spread and my pussy raised, eager to receive his cock. My hands were by my head and my breasts, with their swollen nipples, were pointing straight up. Even through the rubber I could see the throbbing of his cock as the blood pumped into it. He was as tense as I; his eyes carried a mixture of animal excitement and civilized apprehension. We were both breathing rapidly.

He knelt between my legs and guided the head of his cock into the lips of my pussy. Then carefully, slowly, while keeping his cock in exactly the same spot, he stretched over me while supporting himself on his hands, as though he were doing a pushup. Slowly he began to rotate his thighs and work his cock deeper and deeper into my wet and pulsating pussy.

I was afraid it would hurt, and it did. But the pain was not nearly so severe as I had feared, and the concomitant pleasure almost canceled my apprehension and finally subdued it completely. William worked ever more deeply between my thighs until I knew he could go no farther. He paused an instant, the hair of our crotches mingling, then he began to pump, carefully, slowly moving up and down. I grasped his shoulders and lifted my head to search out his lips. The exquisite motion of his thighs grew more rapid and my legs curled around him in an effort to pull him deeper and closer. Our mouths fought for each other; we gasped and licked and our tongues welded as the rhythm of our fucking increased.

With a series of deep thrusts, accompanied by a groan that seemed wrenched from his belly, William's body grew hard as marble, then quivered into softness as he collapsed on top of me. I grasped him, held him pressed closer than I had ever held another human being, and our naked bodies melted into one entity.

I didn't have an orgasm, but I was not disappointed. Like anyone who read women's magazines in the mid-sixties, I was aware that female orgasms had become absolutely necessary for true sexual fulfillment; I knew, because I had masturbated enough to find out, that I was orgasmic. What I hadn't realized, though, was how excruciatingly erotic the touch of another human being on almost any part of my body could be. William's gentle explorations of neck, ear, belly and thigh all set nerves to tingling, and brought on a shuddering network of fulfillment. No, I did not miss the orgasm, not at all.

William lay on top of me for a long while, his cock still in my pussy, our sweat gluing us together as it dried in the warm September air. I cradled his head on my shoulder, stroking his hair, running my fingers over his back, hugging him to me. He roused himself after a while, and carefully retrieved his cock; I felt it leave with regret. He rolled off me, onto his side, and looked at me—much as he had when we first lay down together.

As I watched him, our fingers intertwined. I was suffused with an emotion so strong and satisfying that it blotted out reserve, and I whispered, "I love you, William."

It was the first time—but was not to be the last—that I confused the physical with the emotional, that I thought that surely someone who could make my body feel that good also had dominion over my heart. William also labored under the same misapprehension, for he replied, "I love you, too."

We spent the rest of the afternoon in the small room, hardly ever leaving the narrow bed. The light grew dim as the sun faded, and we continued to touch, caress, explore. We fucked twice more. The last time was so relaxed and gentle, so without tension, that I don't understand today why I didn't come; I suppose I was still more tense than I realized. But, as I said, I didn't miss the orgasm, did not feel deprived or frustrated. On the contrary, on that day a whole new frontier of experience had been opened to me.

William also made a few discoveries that day, I think. Although he was an "older man," and was supposedly the experienced partner, I doubt that he had fucked that much before he fucked me. We never discussed it, but now I suspect that he had

had at most a few jackrabbit encounters that had taught him the rudiments, but none of the refinements, of intercourse. I mistook his innate gentleness and genuine awe of my body as finesse. Quite simply, we were so beautifully matched—our needs so perfectly meshed—that our experience that afternoon was much more glorious than it had any right to be. Even what might have been drawbacks turned into advantages. His shyness made him cautious and gentle, and my inexperience made me, in a curious sense, adventurous. Once, for example, after he had tickled my nipples into tingling erectness, I reciprocated by putting my mouth to his and gently sucked first one then the other while he, astonished, tried (but not very hard) to stop me. I didn't know that men weren't supposed to find their nipples a turn-on and, indeed, I had William twisting with pleasure. Different parts of the body have vogues, I've noticed, and it's only been recently that men have allowed themselves pleasure through their nipples. On that autumn day in 1967, in a Yale dormitory, I did a little trailblazing out of sheer ignorance.

I didn't want to leave. I wanted to stay there forever. The football game had long been forgotten, as well as the party. What finally roused us was hunger; we suddenly discovered ourselves to be famished, after about six hours of fucking. Nothing would do but that we must eat immediately. We were hollow, weak from hunger. Laughing, touching, bumping into each other, we quickly dressed and drove to a restaurant on the edge of

New Haven and had hamburgers—two apiece—with French fries and milk shakes.

Afterwards, there was no question of returning to his room, for I had to leave in order to get home by midnight. Our leave-taking was subdued and gentle; following an afternoon of stretching nakedly side by side, I would have felt silly to try to inject passion into farewell kisses conducted in the front seat of a Buick. I drove William to his dorm. We kissed quickly and he got out, and stood at the curb as I drove away.

Chapter 3

One of the most precious—and most insidious—things I carried away from that afternoon with William was the illusion that all sex was tender, loving, gentle and fulfilling. Even later, when I learned, over and over, how untrue this was, I still behaved as though that experience was the norm, and anything that departed from it was flawed or inauthentic. For several years, I used my first experience as a standard against which I measured all others, and William as an impossibly gleaming arbiter of what was sexually perfect. Hardly anyone, of course, ever measured up; even William, in subsequent meetings, seemed sometimes to fall short.

Another illusion fostered by my first fuck was that it made me mature. I suppose there must be a few things in the world more obnoxious than a sixteen-year-old girl who is certain she knows it all, but I doubt if you could convince my parents of that. I became impossibly independent, rebelling at every suggestion and effort at guidance. Adolescence is, of course, a notoriously stormy period, and mine reached hurricane proportions.

For the next year I saw William whenever I

could, which was not very often. I wasn't able to get to Yale, nor he to come home every weekend; I had my parents to contend with, and he had his studies. He was a serious, ambitious boy, and he would not allow romance to interfere with his grades. He was determined to graduate in the top ten percent of his class. He did, and applied for and was accepted by Stanford in California. This was a blow to me, followed almost immediately by the transferral of his father to another division of his firm in Michigan, so that William no longer had any geographical ties to my part of the country. Though we promised to find a way to be together, though we swore we loved each other (I more ardently than he), within eighteen months the affair was over.

I can talk about that period calmly now, but how devastating it was then! I fluctuated between rage and adoration, tenderness and indifference, and hate and love. I was absolutely impossible, but in explanation—if not excuse—I can say that I really did suffer a great deal. My insecurity was always gnawing at me, pushing me both to gather and disregard reassurance. People could not convince me I was worthwhile, but at the same time I could not stop making them try.

My parents became concerned about my future as my grades in high school began to crumble under the weight of my emotional life. "You'd better be careful, young lady," said my father, in one of his sternest lectures, "or you'll find yourself unable to get into any decent college."

"I don't care," I replied. "I don't need college."

"Oh, Diane," said my mother sadly, "of course you need college. What are you thinking about?"

I would have disputed anything. "I do not need college," I repeated dramatically, "because I'm going to be a model."

This stunned them. The admission threw me off, also, because it just came out. Deep in my heart I knew I could never be a model, because in spite of all the growing evidence to the contrary, I remained convinced I was still ugly, tall, skinny Diane: Beanpole and Jugs. But once I was committed to this course, I defiantly kept to it.

I was still writing to William then, and I told him my decision with the same bravado I had made the announcement to my parents. He took it seriously, as he took everything, and telephoned.

"That's terrific, Diane," he said. "You'll make it."

"Do you really think so?" I asked, both skeptical and wanting to be reassured.

"Absolutely. You're the most beautiful girl I've ever seen. Anywhere. If you want to be a model, I know you can do it."

After William left I gradually started seeing other boys—older men, some of whom I had met through him. I no longer would even look at the boys my own age, nor did I have anything more to do with high school than to attend classes—reluctantly, indifferently, even with hostility. My grades, my last year, were miserable.

When anyone asked me what I was going to do, I'd say, "Oh, I'm not sure. I might try modeling."

The reaction was never surprise or disbelief, though some would be more encouraging than others. "Gee, that's great," or a variation, was the usual reply. Most of the men I was seeing then, I think, liked the idea of dating even a would-be-model.

Yet I did nothing about it. After I graduated, I knew I should go to New York and try, but I didn't have the courage. I had been difficult while in high school—and after I got out I became impossible. I'm still grateful to my parents for putting up with me as long as they did. I didn't want to continue living with them, but I had no means to go elsewhere. They would have supported me if I'd gone to New York, or would have sent me to college, or even to secretarial school, but what they couldn't accept was supporting me while I, paralyzed by insecurity and confusion, did absolutely nothing.

After a discussion—which I considered an argument—I flounced out of the house and drove to the next town, where I took a job as a waitress in a topless bar. Spite was my motivation. "They want me to make something of my life," I said to myself as I drove along the highway, "then I'll make something of myself all right."

The owner of the bar, Jerry Hasket, was a harassed, messy little guy who was thoroughly decent to me. His was one of the first topless bars in the state, and he was nervous about how it would go over and how lenient the authorities would be.

"You sure you don't wanna dance?" he asked wistfully when I applied for the waitress job.

"No," I said, swathed in a chilling dignity. "I just wish to be a waitress."

"Well," he replied, speculatively, "I suppose you'd give the place a little class. You'd have to learn how to bartend, too, so you could spell the regulars during their breaks. . . ."

"That would be fine," I said, my nose in the air. I was patronizing and arrogant—two traits I usually assume when I'm feeling least sure of myself. "When shall I start?"

"How about tonight?"

I did.

For the next five years I worked at the Lovebirds—named after two sad-looking, molting parakeets in a cage at the bar, who died after the first month and were never replaced. There were four waitresses, two bartenders and six dancers—all women, and we worked in shifts. The bartenders and waitresses had skimpy black costumes vaguely modeled on those worn by Playboy Club Bunnies, only the floppy ears were replaced by a feathered headband (because we were lovebirds). I had never met anyone like my coworkers before. They were mostly girls my mother would have called "from the wrong side of the tracks." I guess they were a fairly tough bunch, but after our initial wariness wore off, I became friendly with most of them. There was a high turnover among the dancers as the year wore on, and several times Jerry tried to persuade me to replace one or another girl who didn't show up for her shift. I wouldn't. I was already a little frightened at myself for what I was doing, and to dance topless would have been more than I could have coped with. My parents were horrified, then hurt, when I told them I had become a waitress in a bar. Mother cried, and I was afraid Father was going to. I, myself, felt guilty; yet, I see now, that I took the job as a way of making myself feel superior. I needed to boost my ego by putting myself in a position where I would appear to have the upper hand. If I'd gone to college, or New York, or modeling school, I would have been on a par with everyone else, and I was too insecure to meet the world on equal terms; I had to put myself in a situation which was loaded in my favor. I always kept myself separate from the other girls, watched my language and grammar, and generally made certain that everyone was aware of the difference between me and them.

I was, I suppose, a pain in the ass, but Jerry liked me—"You're weird, but you're classy," he'd say—and eventually trusted me enough to make me a full-time bartender. After a year, I was making good money, and I got my own apartment in the same town where I worked. I was, finally, on my own.

When the Lovebirds closed, after five years, because of some sort of tax trouble I never did understand, I was a bartender with a reputation for being both "a great kid" and "sort of a kook." I had become, in fact, a local celebrity of a minor sort, and I had several offers when word got out I needed a job.

It was, I knew, time for me to move on. If I was going to be a model, I'd have to make an effort. Or I'd have to decide to go to school, or to get married. Bartending was for me what being drafted into the army was for a lot of boys: it was a way of putting off any decisions about what I was going to do with my life.

I recognized this, vaguely, but when the offer came to take over as principal bartender at the Tic-Tac Room in the town's biggest hotel, I accepted with a shrug. I imagine I'd be there still if it hadn't been for one of those chance meetings that always seem so unlikely when you hear about them, yet so inevitable when you experience them.

It was August, around six o'clock in the evening, and I was behind the bar taking care of the few regular drinkers who stopped by on their way home from work. There was a convention of insurance salesmen staying in the hotel—a small group that had not been particularly hard drinkers, so I had not seen much of them. A woman I didn't know came in and sat at the bar. I sized her up immediately as someone's wife, an educated, self-assured, well-groomed attractive brunette in her late twenties or maybe early thirties, with a deep tan and white teeth.

"Is it all right for me to sit at the bar?" she asked me pleasantly. "I'm waiting for my husband." She was friendly and at ease; probably from the West, I thought.

"You bet," I said. "Would you like something while you wait?"

"Oh, I guess a glass of white wine."

A couple of the regulars were giving her the eye, and I decided to put a stop to that. "OK, you guys, this lady's waiting for her husband, so if you've got any ideas, forget 'em, because I'm gonna make sure she waits in peace." I said this lightly, flirtatiously, with a big smile, as was my style. I turned to the woman and added, "Sisterhood is powerful, isn't that right?"

She laughed. "It sure is," she said, and she also smiled at the two guys—pleasantly, without any come-on. The atmosphere became casual and friendly, the kind I created all the time, one reason for my popularity.

Other customers came in, and we joked as we always did, with slightly off-color little quips. "Hey, Diane you forgot the cherry in my drink." "Now, Joe, you know that if I had a cherry left, you could have it." That sort of thing. I made sure the language never got too strong, nor the innuendoes veered from the mildly risqué to the downright vulgar.

"Diane," called the woman, whose name she had told me was Helen. "I'd like you to meet my husband."

I walked down with a big smile, my hand held out to take his, and froze. His jeans replaced by a conservative suit, his hair shorter, his beard gone—there stood William.

Whether he was as surprised as I, I never knew. He didn't lose his composure, but took my hand with every appearance of delight and said, "Diane! What are you doing here?"

His question hit me with the force of a blow. It had been ten years since that afternoon in his dorm room where we had made love. I had left that room certain that I was grown-up and that my life had begun. Yet I had put myself on a top shelf in this inaccessible little closet of a town, making sure that

I would remain unfound and untouched by experience. It was as though I had spent the last ten years in hiding, and suddenly William had come and found me.

"Well, hi!" I said brightly. "Long time, no see!" My belly was as hollow as a drum.

"My gosh." He turned to his wife. "Diane was one of the first people I met after Dad moved to this part of the country."

"That's right," I said, still lively and bright, grinning like some good-time girl who's just been given a free drink.

"Oh really?" said Helen, looking from one to the other of us, polite, and more reserved than she had been a few moments before.

"I've thought about you a lot," said William without any guile. "Every time I opened a magazine I expected to find you there." To Helen, he said, "Diane's a model. Or was going to be." He looked at me quizzically. "How'd that work out?"

"Oh, you know, I got a little sidetracked," I said, laughing.

"I can't believe someone hasn't snapped you up," said William. "Did you go to New York?"

"Well, no, as a matter of fact, I never did make it that far."

"Well, you still look terrific. Doesn't she look great?" he asked his wife.

"Absolutely," said Helen with more enthusiasm than I could have mustered if I'd been in her place.

"Well, thanks," I said, "I can use all the testimonials I can get." Then, before he could ask anything else, I said, "What about you? Did you finally become a lawyer?"

"Yes," he said. "I got out of Stanford and went right to work with a firm in New York. I haven't made partner yet—but soon."

"Well how about that! That calls for a drink on the house. What are you having, William?"

He looked at his wife's glass and said, "White wine, I guess. Thanks." It was plain that neither was much of a boozer. "Listen," he said as I was pouring his drink, "why don't you have dinner with us tonight? I've just remembered . . ." he turned to Helen, "Barry Boston. Maybe he could do something."

Helen didn't look as though she was particularly pleased at the direction the evening was taking, but gamely she covered by saying, "Umm. That's a thought," and smiled at me.

"Now, now," I said in a mock bossy voice, "I don't want to horn in on your evening. Two's company."

"No, really, Diane," insisted William, "we'd love to have you for dinner, and it might be that we can put you in touch with someone who can help you get started."

I didn't want to have dinner with William and his wife; I didn't want to see them ever again. Already, after these few minutes, I felt shaken and shabby. As a bartender with an eccentric reputation, I had managed to build a wall of security and assurance around myself. William threatened to demolish that wall by dragging out all the possibilities—both material and emotional—that once existed. I might have been a model, I might have been famous, I might have had love affairs that were as tender and meaningful as had been promised by that first afternoon with the man now standing before me. Might have. Instead I had settled for a rather tawdry local fame, and a series of encounters with random men who summoned only physical reactions from me, and left no lasting trace on my feelings. I had settled into this ooze of ordinariness, and didn't want to be disturbed.

William, however, wouldn't take no for an answer. "We're staying here in the hotel. What time do you get off?"

"Eight." I had just by chance taken the early shift that afternoon.

"Well, then, why don't we pick you up here at eight?"

"No," I said, "I'll have to go by my place first. Let's say I'll meet you between eight-thirty and nine in the lobby." I wanted to go home and change into my best dress, put on my best perfume, wear my prettiest jewelry—in short, I had to bolster my ego against this attack. I didn't want to see them, but I didn't know how to keep saying no without being surly. So I decided I'd meet them wearing all my defenses.

And I did. When I showed up in the lobby I could see William's eyes widen in admiration, and Helen sized me up with that well-bred wariness wives have when a really beautiful woman appears on the scene.

"Oh wow, Diane," said William. "I guess I couldn't see you very well back there in the bar.

You know, you're actually prettier now than you were when I first met you."

I laughed modestly and winked at Helen conspiratorially, as though we had a little joke between us. "What you see is the result of a little soap and water and a new lipstick."

Helen smiled coolly. She could tell I had gone to a hell of a lot more trouble than a quick shower and a dab of make-up.

The evening turned out to be not as bad as I had feared. I got the conversation going and kept it away from me by asking about William and Helen. He had met her at Stanford and they had married as soon as he'd graduated from law school. Helen was from California, and this was her first time on the East Coast; she liked it well enough, but wanted to return to the West, and it looked as though William might be transferred in a few months. They were on a little weekend jaunt through New England so Helen could see what it looked like. I learned this in bits and pieces through drinks and appetizers; one took over for the other, finishing each other's sentences, laughing and teasing. At one point the bland friendliness among us sparked into something warmer. Helen mentioned that she played tennis and I asked her where; she started telling me about the tennis clubs in New York. I glanced at William for an instant and he was staring at me with such intensity that I felt a blush creep up my throat. Our eyes met in that way only once that evening, and for the briefest second, but it was enough to tell me that he was not as indifferent to our past as I had thought. I don't think Helen noticed.

With the main course, I became the unwilling focus of their attention, as William started talking about breaking into modeling.

"My roommate for a while at Stanford was Barry Boston. You ever hear of him?"

I hadn't.

"Well, he's not very well known, but he's pretty good, I think. A photographer. Fashion mostly, though he does other things too, and he could get you set up."

I shrugged in a self-deprecatory way.

"No, I mean it, Diane. You're a hell of a lot better-looking than most models. If you met the right people I think you could get to the top."

"It's probably a little late for that now."

"Nonsense. You're only . . . how old? Twenty-six?"

"Darling," Helen interrupted, laughing, "that's not a nice question to ask a lady."

"I don't mind," I said, laughing with her. "Yeah. Twenty-six. I think that's considered a little long in the tooth."

"That's not true," said William seriously.

"I do think," said Helen carefully, "that most models I've heard about start in their late teens."

"Most girls, but there are always exceptions," insisted William. "I think Diane is an exception. Just look at her!"

I blushed. William was admiring and Helen was noncommittal as they both stared at me.

"Look," continued William after a few seconds, "I'll give Barry a call. If I set up a meeting will you go see him? It'd just take a day for you to get to the city. Now, how about it?"

Again Helen interrupted. "Darling, don't bully her." She said it lightly, smiling at me, but she was annoyed.

I was embarrassed, but also gratified. I felt reckless and admired, and at the same time, I was afraid that all this attention was undeserved. I smiled at them both, took a deep breath and said, "I don't see how I could turn down an offer like that. Sure I'll go see your friend, if you can arrange it."

William lifted his wine glass. "Here's to the beginning of your career as a model."

Helen, still smiling, took a sip from her glass and said, neutrally, "Here's to your success."

"Thank you, both of you," I said.

We finished dinner and I refused their offer for a nightcap and went home feeling uneasy and elated. I both wanted and feared a change in my life. On the one hand, I said to myself that probably nothing would ever come of William's plan, that he was just carried away for old time's sake and would forget all about our conversation once he returned to New York. On the other hand, I allowed myself to hope that indeed I was going to be whisked into the milieu I had always fantasized about and had never had the courage to approach. I thought, life can happen just like books; maybe people can just step into someone else's life and change things.

Two days later I got a call from William, telling me he had made an appointment for me with Barry Boston for the following week.

Chapter 4

After receiving the offer to get my mango eaten, being recognized by the cab driver and fawned over by the doorman, I felt revived as I entered my uptown studio, which was also my apartment. The studio was cluttered with people: my three assistants, four models, editors from *Fashion* magazine, a make-up man and a wardrobe girl. The latter was somewhat of a joke, since I was scheduled to shoot a feature on fall shoes and patterned stockings, so all she had to do was make sure there were two of everything and that the shoes were polished. Three of the models were girls and one was a boy who was bare to the waist. He was the one the make-up man had to work on, since his was the only face that would show in the layout. I had dreamed up the idea with the *Fashion* editors to do a feature on fall shoes as seen from the angle of a foot fetishist. All we would show would be the shoes and a little stockinged leg, each one being shoved in the face of this guy who was going absolutely bonkers with ecstasy. After some argument, they bought it.

"It's so kinky, Diane," said one editor.

"Maybe, but it'll get attention."

"Well, I suppose we can go along. But I wonder where you get these ideas. . . ."

I smiled. I had gotten the idea the week before from a guy who had spent the evening going bonkers while I shoved my feet in his face.

"Hi, Diane," said my principal assistant, a tall boy from Texas named Jed. He wanted to be a photographer and was learing from the bottom up, just as I had. "Everyone's here. Do you want me to get the first shot set up?"

"Hi. Yeah. Let's do the shot with all three girls around the guy. Tell them to get ready while I slip into my work clothes, will you?" I bustled efficiently into my bedroom to change into coveralls. When doing regular work, I liked to look a little dowdy. It made everyone forget I was still a model myself, and consequently they gave me more respect.

When I came out, Jed had the models assembled in the shooting area, a white-floored square with a roll of white paper pulled down in back. There were two back-up lights and two umbrella lights focused on the center, and my portrait Polaroid was on its tripod aimed in the same direction. Jed and the other two assistants stood by, one with my two Nikons, and another holding a large panel between one of the umbrella lights and the camera in order to keep the glare out of the lens. Jed tested with a light meter and a flash strobe while I bent over the Polaroid to focus the shot.

"Now, I want you three girls to stand in a circle, your left feet forward, your right back—like that. That's right. Now you, Bert, lie down on the floor with your cheek to the ground and stick out your tongue."

There was some giggling as the girls—tousled hair, cut-off jeans, elegant hose and shoes—jockeyed into position. Bert, the male model, was a well-built All-American boy-next-door type. I had chosen him because he looked so wholesome. Just like me.

We did the test shot, and while I was waiting for it to develop, one of the models said, "How come you've started working on the other side of the camera? Are you going to give up modeling?" She was very young, maybe no more than seventeen, but her eyes were calculating beyond her years. In a subtle way she was challenging. I was familiar with her type.

"No."

There was an uneasy pause and another model giggled nervously and said, "Anyone'd be a fool to give up being the Bin-Bin Bead Girl."

"Yeah," said the first girl, whose name, I remembered, was Bette, "that was real lucky." Her tone was snotty, and I had a brief twinge of regret that I wasn't shooting more than her feet: I'd be able to make her look like a mud fence if I could do her face.

"Oh," said the other girl, nervously conciliating, "I'm sure more than luck was involved." Politely to me she asked, "How long were you working before you landed that job?"

"A couple of years," I said curtly. The Polaroid had developed. "There's a hot spot there," I said to Jed. "Adjust the left light. . . ." The shooting got under way.

A couple of years wasn't quite true. It had been four years since I had walked into Barry Boston's studio, apprehensive, excited, miserable with uncertainty and elated with possibilities. I had gone over that meeting in my mind dozens of times before I got there, anticipating everything that would go wrong, preparing for rejection (an outraged "You think *you're* a model?" was one remark I imagined hearing from the imaginary Barry Boston). Of course I was wrong. Reality is never as bad—or as good—as we imagine.

I arrived at his studio exactly on time, eight o'clock on a Thursday evening. He had explained, in a slow, mellow voice, that he would be shooting during the day, but he'd be able to meet me for an hour or so after he'd finished. He had not sounded particularly enthusiastic, but rather bored and uninterested. I almost decided not to keep the appointment because I was so certain he would take one look and ask me to leave.

I wasn't reassured by the location of his studio. It was in the West Thirties of Manhattan, surrounded by once grand office buildings that had deteriorated into lofts for small-time manufacturers. The street was littered with Styrofoam cups, scraps of paper, and overflowing bins of trash. During the day it was obviously crawling with activity, but at five to eight in the evening, as I pulled into a parking spot, it was eerily deserted.

I rang the bell beside Barry Boston's name, and after a few minutes, over the intercom, came the same low voice I'd heard on the phone: "Who is it?"

"Diane Bourne," I said, through pinched lips.

There was a long pause, during which I both feared and hoped that he'd decided not to let me in. Then he said, as slowly as cold molasses, "Great. Come on up," and buzzed.

In the elevator I pushed the button that had "Barry Boston" printed by it, and it rose creakily until the door opened onto the whole fourth floor. It was my first sight of a photographer's studio, and in my mood, and that light, it looked as spooky as the far side of the moon. He had three umbrella lights spaced on a stark white square of floor, and a large old-fashioned fan on a stand nearby.

Overhead, on a heavy pipe framework, there were huge rolls of paper, something for a giant's butcher counter, in white and black and red and purple, the ends dangling at various lengths, and floating in the draft of an open window. Off to one side there was a pile of fabrics and pillows—chiffons and silks and puffy squares of violent primary colors. In the dim light I looked hard at the mass, for intertwined with the scarves and downy poufs was a slender nude, immobile woman lying on her stomach, looking as though she had been tossed there as lightly as one of the scraps of material. There was a strong scent of incense and something else heavy in the air.

From the back of the loft came the slow, low musical voice: "Hey, Diane baby, glad ya could come," and Barry Boston drifted out of the shadows.

Barry Boston was one of those people who never managed to escape the sixties, and not just the sixties but the California sixties. He was—and still is—cool and laidback to the point of parody. He ambled toward me, a detached smile on his face, a joint held out in greeting. He was not quite as tall as I, but with a good build (the only kind California seems to export—I assume they throw the imperfect specimens into the Pacific) and black curly hair frizzed out around his face. His mustache and beard were neatly trimmed into a style I would now call modified rebel, but then found intimidatingly debonair. He wore only beach pants made out of parachute silk dyed khaki, with no shoes, and three strings of beads and feathers across his hairy chest.

In contrast to his casual manner, his eyes were shrewd and watchful, and they flicked over my face and body as quickly as a lizard's tongue. "So, you're a friend of old William's," he said affably.

"That's right," I replied with a prim smile. I was disoriented by the studio, by the naked girl asleep on the pile of red, blue and yellow rags, and by the handsome but weird creature thrusting a skinny joint under my nose. Barry was a little older than William—I'd say about thirty-three or four—and from the other side of the world. I didn't know how to react, arriving in his lair from my Connecticut hotel bar where someone like him would have been asked to leave, if not arrested. So I became frostily polite. "What a nice place," I said, ignoring his offer of the joint.

"Yeah. Lemme get you some wine." He took my hand and led me toward the back of the loft, which was where he lived in a conversation pit surrounded by dozens of plants in large clay pots. "Have a seat, babe, and I'll be right with you." He ambled over to the unwalled kitchen and opened the refrigerator door, which cast a sharp ray of light into the general gloom. I became aware of electronic music whining and beeping softly into the twilight.

I sat gingerly on the long foam built-in couch; it was impossible not to look, and I felt open to attack. Barry handed me a stemmed glass of red wine, then sank beside me. He put his hand on my shoulder and said, "So you're gonna break into modeling?"

"Yes. Well, at least I want to try."

"That's cool." He massaged my shoulder a moment, staring dreamily at my face. "You got experience, babe?"

"No."

He cupped my chin in his hand and turned my face to the left and right, gently but firmly, his black eyes appraising. "You know, babe, you might have something. How do you photograph?"

"Well, I look OK in snapshots, I suppose."

"Uh huh." He stroked my arm, while gazing speculatively over my head. "Well, let's see how you show up in something more than snapshots. You bring any clothes?"

"I beg your pardon?"

"Any changes? Any costumes?"

"Well, no, I didn't know . . ."

"That's OK. I'll get you something." He walked up front to the nest of rags on which the nude was sleeping and pulled out a flimsy-looking red piece of material. It was a gauzy kimono. "Let's start with this. You can change over there." He pointed to an arch, which turned out to be the bathroom with a sunken tub in the center and a toilet in an alcove. There was no door.

I stood for an instant with the flimsy, wide-sleeved garment in my hand, debating whether to change or get the hell out of there. Then I thought that I had made the trip, I had promised William I'd go through with it . . . and what could that doped-up flake do to me anyway? Quickly I took off my blue pantsuit and was debating whether to leave on my bra and panties when Barry appeared in the door.

"Take off everything, babe, before you put that red thing on. You bring any make-up?"

"Yes."

He wandered out of sight, and I stripped naked and put on the gauzy red robe. In the mirror over the sink, I could see my nipples through the material unless I bunched it up, which I tried to do. I powdered my face, freshened my lipstick and put some blush on my cheeks. Then I carefully combed my hair.

"What's keeping you?" he called from the front.

With a sigh I stepped out of the bathroom.

The white square was blazing with all the lights turned on and the white backdrop paper pulled to the floor. Barry had placed a plain wooden stool in the center, and he was adjusting a camera on a tripod to aim at it.

"Just hop up on that seat, babe," he said,

barely glancing at me before he returned to the sight.

I sat on the stool gingerly, making sure there was a double fold of material over my breasts.

"Hold it." There was a blinding flash. "That's just to see how the lights are," he said conversationally. He came over and studied my face. Gone was the woozy gaze. He would have looked at a rock with the same dispassion. "That's a lousy job of make-up," he said. "You're gonna have to do something about that one of these days." He then went to the table where he had put the film to develop and pulled it out. "Umm. OK. We'll get started with a few face shots."

He picked up another camera, attached a long cord to it, and said, "Look straight at me," and pushed the button. The strobe flash exploded into brilliance, and kept exploding for the next hour as Barry talked me into one pose after another.

"Loosen up, babe. Have some more wine. Now smile . . . just a little . . . that's it. Now give me a pout . . . oh, is she ever mad . . . pucker the lips, steam in the eyes . . . you are not happy . . . that's right. . . . Now lean forward . . . further . . . uh, huh, hold it. . . .

"Take some Kleenex, there at your feet, and blot the sweat off . . . now lower the top, more . . . let's see a little bit of tit . . . uh huh . . . now more tit . . . gimme right down to the nipple. . . ."

I tightened. "Just what kind of pictures are you taking?" I asked haughtily, clutching the robe to my throat.

Still holding the camera, he walked over and

pulled the gown off my shoulders and lowered my hand so that my breasts were all but naked. "This is no time for a Mary Poppins act, babe. Let's get on with it." His apparent indifference to me as anything but an object stunned me into acquiescence. I left my hand where he had placed it, and my breasts uncovered.

I resented him, but at the same time wanted to please him. As the session wore on, I also began to feel curiously caressed by the camera as Barry hovered and crouched and moved to and fro, exploring me with its lenses. The lights were warm and I had to keep blotting the sweat from my face and breasts. Barry was sweating also, but he just wiped his forearm across his brow and kept on clicking.

"How much you weigh, babe?" he asked as he worked.

"One twenty-five, about."

"You're gonna have to lose some weight. The camera says you weigh one thirty-five, maybe one forty. Now hold it . . . lean forward . . . let the tits hang . . . that's right . . . stay there and look up . . . uh huh. . . ." He pushed my hair back, and his touch made me catch my breath. He brought the camera so close it was focused only on my lips and neck. "Wet the lips and hold 'em open . . . wetter . . . that's right . . . show me some tongue, just the tip . . . that's right . . . now hold your hand right there by your tits . . . spread your fingers . . . wider. . . ."

I became aware that I was breathing heavily, and a musky scent rose off my body like mist from a swamp. Barry kept probing with the camera: "Now spread your fingers over your tits, wider and wet your lips again . . . uh huh . . . you got nice hands, babe, you could do parts."

"What?"

"Parts. Shots of your hands . . . with rings, things like that. Hold it."

I kept my hands across my breasts, my palms lightly grazing my nipples. The robe dropped but I made no effort to pull it back up. I was willing to do anything Barry Boston told me to do. He—and his camera—were like a lover fondling me with charged fingers.

My senses became constricted to the brilliant white square and the rhythmic explosions of the strobe flash, so I was jarred when a small, petulant voice from beyond the boundary said, "Barry? What's happening?" I glanced at the pile of rags and saw a thin, blonde girl with tiny perfect breasts sitting cross-legged on top of them. Her hair had been carelessly gathered to the crown of her head, and wispy tendrils floated beside her narrow face. She looked at me out of chary eyes.

"Hey," said Barry, his camera still focused on me. "You decide to come to the party?"

"I fell asleep," she said accusingly, watching us the way a kitten observes unexpected movement.

"Surprise," said Barry, turning to her. "You always fall asleep when you eat on top of a qualude."

"Half a 'lude," she said poutingly.

"Half a 'lude and six brownies . . . enough to knock anyone out." He walked over and lightly massaged her head. "Meet Diane. Diane, this is Cissie."

"How do you do?" I said, as formally as anyone who has just pulled a swatch of red gauze over her naked breasts could.

"Hi," said Cissie, looking at me cautiously. She was very young, probably no more than seventeen. She looked up at Barry standing over her, entwined his legs with both arms, and put her cheek to his thigh. "Was I out for long?"

"Just long enough for me and Diane to get acquainted," he said teasingly, and smiled at me.

I returned his look impassively, not knowing whether to be compliant or glacial. I opted for trying to be nothing at all—a cipher. Cissie, still holding Barry's leg with one arm, ran her hand possessively over his crotch while staring at me. Through the silk of his beach pants, I saw the outlines of his semi-hard cock.

"Are we finished?" I asked, businesslike.

"Ummm. I don't think we ought to call it quits just yet. Maybe we can take a break," Barry said, as he continued to stroke Cissie, bending a little so that he almost reached her breast. She kept her hand in his crotch, cradling his balls beneath the silk.

I sat on the stool, back erect, my face composed into an expression of polite indifference. I thought about getting dressed, but that, I feared, would look too prissy, as though I were censuring them. Above all, I did not want to appear unsophisticated, like a hick visiting the big city. And, though I barely acknowledged it, I was still excited by my encounter with the camera, which had given rise to anticipations I would have liked to satisfy. So I sat, a small smile on my face.

Cissie, whether through defiance or indifference to my presence, reached up and untied the drawstring to Barry's beachpants. They slithered down over his now hard cock and down his legs to form a puddle of khaki silk at his feet. She ran her fingers up and down his hairy inner thigh, then lightly bit him just above the knee.

"Oh, wow," said Barry dreamily, looking down at her. "I ought to feed you more brownies."

She rose to her knees and raised her mouth to take his balls in it, while his cock rested on her turned-up forehead.

"Easy . . . easy . . . ," crooned Barry. "No teeth, baby. . . ."

With both hands she cupped his ass and pulled his crotch closer to her mouth. His cock was circumcised, neat, symmetrical and well designed, like the rest of him. Cissie ran her tongue over the undershaft of it, then put its head in her mouth.

Barry sucked in his breath as though he were inhaling port. "Ahhhh," he said, and held her by the hair with both hands while he gently undulated back and forth, fucking her face.

Barry and Cissie were talkers. I've always taken sex silently, but I've run into the occasional guy who likes to forecast everything he's going to do, describe everything he's doing, then discuss everything he's done. Barry and Cissie belonged to that ilk.

"Ohhh, baby, open your throat, and swallow that cock. You like that cock?"

"Ummm," said Cissie.

"You want more?"

"Umm."

"Here it comes. You ready for it baby?"

"Umm."

"I don't wanna shoot yet." He slid his cock out of her mouth and rubbed it, shiny with spit, against the side of her face. Still holding her hair with both hands, he sank, rubbing his cock over her shoulders, between her breasts, down her belly, until they were both on their knees facing each other. He wrapped his arms around her waist and pulled her closer, while his cock emerged from between her legs behind her.

Still I remained perched on the stool, like an observant owl on a tree branch. My first concern, foolishly, was to keep my dignity; I did not want to be gauche or awkward, and I could think of no action that would not jeopardize my image. If I had more self-assurance, such a concern would never have come up—but I did not. And there was another factor: I would have liked to participate. I had never taken part in a three-way scene, but I had had fantasies. I was hot from my bout with the camera, and Barry turned me on. If there had been an invitation I would have accepted it, but they seemed to ignore me (though I realize now that, in a sense, I did participate insofar as my presence was important to them). I was unable to hop off my stool and saunter over with a cheery, "Mind if I join you?" I didn't have enough confidence. So I remained, red-robed, in the center of the brilliantly chaste white square, while Cissie and Barry explored each other on the pile of many-hued rags.

"What am I going to do with you, baby?"

whispered Barry.

"You're going to fuck me," said Cissie in a child's voice.

"How'm I going to fuck you?"

"Anyway you want to."

He eased her away from him, so that she lay on her back while he remained on his knees over her, his cock horizontal from his groin. Bending, he took one of her nipples between his teeth and bit hard enough to make her moan and writhe. With his fingers he began to work into her pussy as her legs convulsively spread and closed in jerks.

"You like that?" he asked.

"I like anything you wanna do."

"Anything?"

"Yeah." Her breasts were thrust upward and her hips were raised; her pussy, with its sparse golden hair, was open and as glistening as a bursting, ripe fig.

From a small chest beside the rags Barry pulled out a couple of black objects. He held one in each hand and rubbed them over Cissie's breasts. She watched him, her mouth open, her hands flung back over her head.

"You want the tit clamps, baby?" he asked in a teasing, cajoling voice.

"If you want me to," said Cissie breathlessly.

"Nah. You gotta beg for 'em, baby."

"Let me have the tit clamps."

"Please?"

"Please let me have the tit clamps."

Slowly he glided one, then the other, black metal clamp up to and around Cissie's erect nipples.

He pinched the clamps open, placed them on the nipples, and carefully released them. Cissie groaned, almost whined, and her mouth stretched in a grimace of pain.

"You like that, baby?"

"Yes," she whispered.

Barry leaned over her breasts and blew on them without touching them. His left hand returned to her pussy, and with his right he pulled from the chest a pink plastic vibrator and clicked it on. It purred softly.

"You wanna get fucked, baby?" he asked.

"Yes."

He rubbed the vibrator along her belly. "You want this up your cunt?"

"I want your cock."

"You want my cock up your cunt?"

"Yes." She was thrusting her pussy toward him, supporting herself on her shoulders and heels. She rubbed the open pink lips against his belly and balls.

From the chest Barry took a tiny yellow cylinder and held it near Cissie's nose.

"Take some popper, baby," he said, as he squeezed and broke the vial. I could whiff the amyl nitrate from where I sat. Cissie inhaled as he stuffed the cotton-wrapped ampoule up first one nostril then the other, and her fair skin grew flushed as she stretched and moaned. Then Barry sniffed as deeply as she had while holding the popper to his nose. He opened a jar of Vaseline and dipped the vibrator into it, then smoothed the grease down the shaft. He lightly ran the tip of the vibrator around Cissie's moist pussy, then moved it lower, and slowly shoved it into her ass.

Cissie groaned, her eyes closed, her arms trembling, her legs open and raised, her toes curled downward. "Oh, baby, fuck me," she said, her head twisting from side to side.

Barry took another yellow phial from the chest, snapped it under Cissie's nose and held it there as she sniffed deeply; then he took a hit himself and lowered his body over hers. Without using his hands he guided his cock slowly into her pussy.

Cissie cried out, gasped and threw her head back so far that her throat was a white arc against the brilliant fabrics. "Fuck me," she cried. "Give it to me. All of it."

"It's yours, baby. You like it?" Barry was moving slowly and rhythmically, up and down, his hairy round ass bobbing between her white raised legs.

"Yes," she said, ". . . yes."

He began to move faster and raised his head and clenched his teeth. His eyes were squinted shut, as though he were in pain. He began to moan, a keen, strained sound, as he prodded harder and faster. Cissie threw her arms to his shoulders and pulled at him as she kept repeating, "Fuck me, fuck me, fuck me."

With a deep rapid thrust Barry penetrated as far as he could as Cissie cried, "I'm coming, baby, oh, I'm coming." She pulled on his shoulders so hard she left a red trail across his back.

"I'm gonna shoot, baby," said Barry between clenched teeth. "You're gonna get my load." With a grunt he gave three violent thrusts and collapsed on top of her, his head beside her, their arms outstretched.

They lay still.

Tentatively, I cleared my throat. I felt a little like the teenager who sits on the sidelines during school parties while everybody else dances; at the same time I noted, with a sour satisfaction, that Barry had never once kissed Cissie. I cleared my throat again, and again there was no response from the couple on the rag heap. I got off the stool and went to the bathroom where I changed back into my pants suit and freshened my make-up. I didn't know how to take my leave. Did I slip tactfully away, or nudge Barry into acknowledging my farewell?

I needn't have worried, for when I returned to the studio part of the loft, Barry was getting back into his beach pants. He yawned widely, then smiled at me in what I then considered an arrogant manner, but I now suspect was more inspired by bravado. He made no reference to what had happened, nor did I. Cissie remained immobile on the pile of rags. I remember wondering whether the vibrator was still up her ass and, if so, was it still turned on. I never found out.

"Hey, Diane, you all ready to go?" asked Barry.

"Yes," I said with a pleasant smile, as though nothing had happened.

"I'll have the contacts in a couple of days. You live in the city?"

"No, but I'll be here for a day or so."

"Gimme a call, then, and we'll choose the shots for your portfolio."

"Portfolio?"

"Yeah. You know, so you can show agencies."

"Oh."

He looked more closely at me. "You really are just breaking in, aren't you?"

"Trying to," I said with a self-depracating shrug.

"Well, maybe I can help." He smiled again and led me to the elevator where he kissed the air by my cheek as a good-bye gesture.

"OK, Bert," I said to the half-naked boy on the floor, "now I want you to lie on your back and you," I signaled to the snotty little model, Bette, who had become more and more troublesome as the afternoon progressed, "hold your foot just over his mouth. Stick out your tongue, Bert, try to lick the sole of the shoe. Point the toe down more. . . ."

"I can't hold my balance," said Bette.

"Bring her a stool to lean on," I told Jed.

"How much longer are we going to be?" asked Bette. "I've got another booking in an hour. They're paying cash, too."

I said nothing.

"I really need that booking," she continued, hostility in her voice and eyes. "I don't have a regular gig like Bin-Bin Beads."

I shot one shot and changed my angle to get another.

"I guess I'm just not the wholesome type," she said to the room at large, then gave a nasty little laugh. "Or maybe I don't know the right people."

I snapped another shot.

"Or like they say, maybe it's not who you know, but who you sleep with."

The room was very still as I straightened up. "Or maybe," I said slowly and distinctly, "you're just a pain in the ass." I handed the camera to Jed, then said to Bette, "That's it for you. I don't need you anymore." To the other two models, waiting worriedly on the side, I said, "Both of you come over and stand with your left feet forward and Bert, turn on your stomach and encircle the feet with your arms."

Bette, realizing she had gone too far, hovered on the sidelines, a scared apology just waiting for an invitation to emerge. I ignored her. I was able to, because when I was behind the camera I had the upper hand, a fact that Bette apparently had not yet learned. I had learned it the hard way. So would she, or she'd get out of the business.

Chapter 5

I finished the shoot, and everyone cleared out—the models rushed off; the make-up man packed his case, which looked like a big tool chest; the frumpy editors from *Fashion,* with their smudged lipstick, frizzy hair and wrinkled clothes left; and Jed and my other assistants took the film to the lab. Suddenly it was quiet.

I was restless—the image of Randy Wrong kept warring with my replay of the scene with Bette. Neither memory was conducive to relaxation. I wandered out to my kitchen, with its pink walls, stove, icebox and sink, and made a cup of tea. I carried it to the bedroom and flopped down facing the TV, which I switched on. It was a little after seven-thirty as I watched myself waver into focus in full color. I was walking down a long white staircase—modeled after those stairs in 1930s movies—wearing a red satin dress with a train and six strands of white and red marble-sized beads and a matching five-strand bracelet and dangling earrings. As I descended a careful step at a time, a top-hatted man turned and looked at me ardently. I, however, looked only at the camera as I advanced and, pushing my hair back so the earrings and bracelet would all be in focus with the necklace, I whispered intimately, "Bin-Bin Beads make you *beautiful.*" The music, a pastiche of thirties tunes, swelled as the smitten escort led me off and an invisible male announcer extolled the virtues of Bin-Bin Beads, and explained how, though they looked like a million dollars, they were well within the reach of almost everybody, and so on, and so on.

I looked the way a wholesome girl next door might look on a big night out. Hairdressers and make-up and wardrobe people had worked on me for four hours to get just that image. I regarded the creature on the screen as something that had little to do with me; I was nothing but raw material transformed by experts into a desirable myth.

I sipped my tea as the program accompanying the commercial (which is how I considered it) got under way with its dumb comedy and canned laughter. Gratefully, I switched off the sound when the phone rang, and left the images mutely flickering.

"Hello?"

"Diane? Hi, this is William."

I paused for several beats; it had been at least six months since I had last heard from him. Modestly, he added, "William Allen."

"I know which William," I said laughing. "I'm just glad to hear from you. Are you in town?"

"No, I'm calling from the coast. But I'm coming to New York next week and I have something to talk to you about."

"Terrific. Is Helen coming with you?"

"No. This is strictly a business trip. In fact, it's business having to do with you."

"Oh?"

"Yes. I don't want to talk about it on the phone."

"Give me some idea?"

"Well, you know, I'm consultant to Wade and Thomas . . ."

"How could I forget?" Wade and Thomas was the advertising agency that handled the Bin-Bin Bead account.

"Yes. Well, something has come up about the ads."

"Oh?"

"Look, Diane, I don't want to get into this over the phone but, well, we have to talk about a couple of things."

"Fine," I said. "Whenever you want."

"You'll be in town next week?"

"Sure."

"Then I'll give you a call as soon as I get in."

"I'm looking forward to seeing you again," I said. We hung up.

I stared at the still-animated screen as the witless actors silently mouthed and gesticulated in strained pantomime. The ominous overtones of the conversation had made me uneasy. Then I thought that William was probably exercising his usual lawyer's caution and was, above all, being discreet. I consoled myself with the reassurance that William had always been helpful to me; if there was anyone in the world I could trust, it was him.

Not only had he introduced me to lovemaking

in the most gentle way possible, urged me to try to model, and arranged my first test shots, he had also hovered in the background with advice, help and introductions ever since I had come to New York. Even after he had been transferred to California he had always acted as though I were some sort of ward whose well-being he took personally to heart.

When I had left Barry Boston's studio, for example, after being photographed and then watching Barry perform with Cissie (and a performance is what it was), I was more uncertain than ever about whether to stay in New York or flee back to Connecticut where life was dull, but predictable. I had called William from my hotel room that night, practicing a chirpy, carefree voice before dialing the number.

Helen answered, and when I identified myself she assumed the forced good-natured tone the well-bred take when speaking to someone they'd just as soon not hear from. "Why, Diane," she said, "how are you?"

"Just fine. Terrific," I said in my good-time-girl voice. "I just thought I'd call to let you and William know that I did go to see the photographer."

"How nice. How did it work out?"

"Oh, terrific, just great, really. He's a really nice guy."

"Well, isn't that nice," she said, after a pause.

"I wonder if William's there?" I asked breezily, as though it were an afterthought. "I'd like to thank him for launching my career." I laughed too loudly.

There was another hesitation before Helen said, "Just a second. Let me see if he's busy."

I pictured her making a long trip from phone to some paneled library; actually, they lived in a small apartment in the East Seventies. Within a minute William had picked up the phone.

"Hi, Diane. That's great news." He sounded sincerely pleased. "What's the next step? Did Barry say?"

"Well, I'm going to call him and get the proofs, or contacts, or something like that, and then he said he'd see. I don't know. Something might come of it, or maybe not. But anyway, I wanted to thank you for setting it up."

"My pleasure," said William, friendly and open. I wondered whether Helen was standing at his elbow. "How long are you going to be in town?"

"Oh, only a few days, I suppose, until I see what happens."

"I've got to fly to Los Angeles tomorrow, but when I get back we can get together." There was no hint of any intimacy. It was a friendly invitation from a very married man. "If you need anything while I'm gone, don't hesitate to call Helen," he added.

"Thanks. I'll do that. And I really am grateful, William." We talked a few minutes longer and then hung up. I was a little let down; I had known that only a few pleasantries would come from the conversation, but I had hoped for more. I smiled wryly to myself as I recalled William's urging me to call Helen in case I needed anything. If I were Helen, I thought, I would avoid Diane Bourne like the plague.

Two days later I called Barry Boston, and he

had the contact sheets. He asked me up at eleven o'clock the next morning.

I arrived to find an atmosphere entirely different from the first time I'd been there. There was a crowd: models, hairdressers, make-up men and women, editors and assistants. It was my first glimpse of all those people who are ordinarily involved in a shoot. Barry was different also; he was aloof and lordly in the way he oversaw the activity, approving make-up, hair styles, layouts and backdrops. The actual shoot had not started yet, but the models had been there since eight-thirty, he told me, having their hair and nails done and make-up applied. Barry walked among them like a lion. He still had an aura of the sixties—he was wearing his beads and a loose white Indian shirt over baggy blue jeans—but he was obviously very much in control. He greeted me with a cursory smile. "Let's go to the office," he said, and walked to a door behind the backdrops that I hadn't noticed on my first visit. There, in a small room with a window on an airshaft, was a desk and battered wooden chair with a lambskin thrown over it. There was no chair for me, so I leaned against the desk as Barry took contact sheets out of a large white envelope. There, on several pieces of photographic paper were tiny pictures of me, all running into each other.

All business, he said, "I've circled the ones you ought to get blown up. Do you want to look over the others?"

"Well, if you think you've got the right ones marked . . ."

"I do. There're eight that are good. Really

good. You're going to need a little fixing up, but I think with these you can get into an agency."

I felt a thrill. "You think I can be a fashion model, then?"

"No. You'll never be a fashion model. Even if you had started when you were seventeen or eighteen, which is what you should have done, you couldn't have been a fashion model." He spoke brusquely, not trying to soften his words.

I looked at him, confused and hurt. He had, in a single moment, raised my hopes, then dashed them so thoroughly I couldn't speak.

Still businesslike, he continued. "What you can be is a product model. I can almost guarantee that you'll be taken by a commercial agency, and can also guarantee that no fashion agency will touch you."

I didn't know what he was talking about, but I didn't like what I was hearing. "You mean," I said after an instant, "that I'm not pretty enough to be a real model."

With an impatient shake of his ringleted head he said, "You're a knockout. You're beautiful. That's why I'm taking this trouble with you. I wouldn't have bothered otherwise. Even the fact that you're already old won't stop you. But you're not a *fashion* model. Fashion models have a look that you don't have. That doesn't mean they're prettier than you, it means they're different. You have a look *they* don't have. You've got a great look, and you'll be a great product model." He spoke with finality. Pushing the contacts back into the envelope, he added, "I'll have those eight shots blown up, and then I'll send you over to see Harold Ames."

"Who's that?"

"He owns a commercial agency that's expanding. He has a good head sheet, and I do a lot of work with him."

Things were happening too fast, and I didn't understand. All I could grasp was that Barry was telling me I'd never slink through the pages of *Vogue*, never contort myself into those enticing positions that I had spent so many hours in front of a mirror practicing as a teen-ager back in Connecticut. Maybe, I thought, my dream to be a model was coming true, but it seemed a flawed dream, not nearly so satisfying as it veered toward realization.

I hid my disappointment with the smile I had perfected behind a Connecticut bar and said, "Barry, I really appreciate what you're doing for me. Thanks so much for all the trouble."

He waved me into silence. "It's my business. I do a lot of work with Harold Ames. If I send him good people, he'll send me good people. I think you're worth his looking over, that's all." He gave me an asexual pat on the ass as he stood up, and I could see he was already thinking about something else. As I thanked him again he nodded vaguely, opened the door of his office and stepped into the studio where the setup for the first shot was being prepared. He bent over his Polaroid, no longer aware of my existence, as I got into the elevator.

Two days later Barry messengered the blow-ups to my hotel, and I saw myself smiling, pouting, smoldering, enticing, inviting. I was delighted. With the glossies Barry sent the phone number of Harold Ames and a scrawled note that he had already told him about me. I made an appointment for that afternoon.

The office of the Harold Ames Agency was in the East Fifties and it was another disappointment. The building was one of those anonymous structures that seem to come and go in New York without much fanfare, and the reception room was windowless, small and cramped. There was not a vestige of glamour or sparkle: three grey plastic-padded chairs, a pot of unhealthy ivy, and a grey metal desk behind which sat a pleasant girl about my age, who wore glasses and a denim skirt with a white blouse.

"Hi," she said, when I entered carrying my photographs.

"Hello," I said. "I'm Diane Bourne. I have an appointment with Mr. Ames."

I was still sure that, at some point in the strange series of developing events, someone was going to pop up and tell me to stop fooling myself and go back to the bar in Connecticut where I belonged. So, as usual, my nervousness translated itself into hauteur.

"Oh, yes. Hi. Harold's expecting you." She leaned back to open the door behind her. "Diane's here," she called.

Harold Ames was short and pudgy, with black, longish hair and a shy smile. His tan gabardine slacks were pressed, his brown boots shined, and his white silk shirt was open down to his smooth mid-chest. He held out a welcoming hand, but his brown eyes didn't quite engage mine as he said, "Nice to see you, Diane. Come in." Then to the girl at the desk, "Hold my calls for the next few minutes, will you?"

His office was larger and more comfortable than the reception room, but still not impressive. Two windows, festooned by rust drapes, faced Madison Avenue. His desk was polished cherry wood, and looked antique, and there were two large green easy chairs and a black sofa around a coffee table. He pointed to the sofa and took one of the chairs. "Well, Barry had some good things to say about you."

I was aware that I was being sized up, so I smiled coolly and replied, "That's very kind of him." I crossed my ankles like a debutante.

"Have you got the pictures?" he asked, looking at the envelope. I passed it to him. He opened it and spread the photographs on the coffee table.

"Um hum," he said as his eyes moved from one to the other. "Um hum, very nice." He looked at me—or rather slightly to the left of me—as he said, "Would you walk for me please?"

I hesitated an instant, not sure what was required, before standing and self-consciously walking to the desk and back.

"Um hum" he said. "Now walk and twirl quickly, and walk back, please."

I did so, smiling slightly as though I considered the whole business childish. I was, by that time,very nervous.

"Um hum." He nodded several times before saying, "I think we can work together, Diane." He picked up the pictures and glanced from them to me and added, "You're going to have to lose ten pounds. You've got bones there we have to bring out. Your hair's wrong. It should be cut fuller; I know a good guy for that. You need help with your make-up. I'll send you to someone for that. And we'll need more photographs, but these'll do to start with." He looked me up and down and asked, "How old are you?" I hesitated and he smiled slightly as he said, "About twenty-five, twenty-six?"

"Twenty-six," I said stiffly.

He nodded. "And you're five foot ten?"

"That's right." I was on the defensive.

He didn't seem to notice. "Both your age and height are against you. The height wouldn't be so bad if you were doing fashion, but for product modeling, it'll mean there are some things you won't be able to work with. A lot of manufacturers don't want big girls dwarfing their products." He smiled and shrugged. "As for the age—well, there's work to be had for your age-range; not as much as if you were younger, but there's work out there."

I said nothing. My excitement at being accepted as a model was diluted by the distinctly unglamorous method of acceptance. I sensed that Harold Ames and I were there to discuss some commodity. (My feeling was correct, for in becoming a model, I eventually realized that I had metamorphosed into nothing more nor less than a small business.)

"We handle both print and television, and take twenty percent commission," said Harold Ames briskly.

"Is there something to sign, or anything like that?"

"No. Some agencies have a written agreement, but we don't. You understand that we handle you exclusively?"

"Yes."

"That's all there is to it, then. I'm happy to have you with us." He extended his hand and smiled, but still avoided direct eye contact.

He had the girl at the desk give me the addresses of the hair stylist and make-up men I was to see, and also the phone number of another photographer, in order to have some more pictures made for my portfolio.

A week later I landed my first job. I was the girl holding a bottle of eyewash directly next to my eyes, with the top of my head and the bottom of my face cropped; just my bright eyes and the eyewash were all that showed, but I was paid a hundred dollars an hour, and I was officially a model.

The evening of my first shoot I had dinner with William and Helen. William had returned from Los Angeles and called to ask me to meet them at their apartment for drinks, and then to have dinner in a neighborhood restaurant. When I told him about the shoot he said, "That's great! I always knew you'd make it. We'll have a celebration—a double celebration, because Helen and I have some good news, too."

By this time I had been in New York for a week; I hadn't even returned to Connecticut to close my apartment, but had plunged into the appointments with the hair-stylist, who layered my hair to make it look fuller, and the make-up expert who had, as he put it, "Sculpted the cheekbones with taupe shading, and emphasized the eyes with brown shadow and eyeliner. . . ." He also softened my lips with a coral tint and applied just a hint of apricot blush to the cheeks. When both had finished I still looked like me, but I was a lot more beautiful. I could assess myself objectively; the way, I suppose, an actress who assumes the costume and make-up of a part can look at herself with dispassion. The girl I saw in the mirror was me, but a me who had been glorified by experts.

I also went on a diet, and within the first week lost three pounds with hardly any effort.

So by the evening I whizzed up to the East Seventies to meet William and Helen, I was floating along on a cushion of unaccustomed confidence. I had charged a new dress at Bendel's just for the occasion—a classic navy linen which would make William see only me, and make Helen's eyes narrow in assessment.

Their apartment was the second floor of a brownstone on a pretty tree-lined street. It was small, but chicly simple, with bare gleaming floors and sparse chairs by Mies van der Rohe and Breuer contrasting with an ornate ceiling and fireplace of the last century. It was the perfect setting for Helen, who looked social and composed in a white shirtdress that showed up her tan. Both she and William greeted me warmly, and William, his admiration undisguised said, "Good Lord, Diane. Is this what New York can do to little girls from Connecticut?"

"Not so little," I said, laughing. "For this business I'm too big and pretty well over the hill, but my agent thinks I may have a few kicks left before they put me out to pasture."

"Over the hill at twenty-six," said William, shaking his head. "What a business."

"But you have gotten work?" asked Helen politely.

"Yes," I said self-deprecatingly. "For eyewash. It's a beginning."

"I should say," William cut in. "And after only a week! Fantastic!"

We had drinks, then went to a small French restaurant nearby on Third Avenue—candlelight, checked tablecloths, waiters with accents. Helen and William were very much a couple, and I felt very much a loner. I tried not to let the situation get to me, but I couldn't help feeling awkward. I was careful to divide my attention equally between Helen and William, but it was obvious—certainly to Helen—that I was more interested in her husband than in her. During the meal she sat as close to him as a newlywed.

If William noticed the tension between his wife and me, he didn't let on. Rather, he guided the conversation along pleasantly bland paths, and then with the main course broke his good news.

"I've just joined Harper and Cohn, and it's certain I'll be a partner within five years or so. *And*—this is what makes Helen so happy—" he winked and patted her hand; I smiled with my lips, "we're going to be moving to California, because most of the work is out there."

"Well, isn't that nice," I said, as William and Helen beamed.

"Actually," William continued, "our paths may cross professionally, because Harper and Cohn handles a lot of advertising agencies—particularly TV agencies. That's why I'm being sent to the coast. It's a big move for me. For us." He smiled at his wife.

"I'm truly happy for you, William," I said, "and you, too, Helen." I was disappointed, yet I couldn't have put a specific cause to it at that instant. Later, however, as we were choosing dessert, I glanced up and found William studying me over the menu. He held my eyes for a long moment before dropping them and saying, "Oh, I think I'll just have coffee."

"Me too," I said. I looked at him, hoping to catch his glance again, but he seemed absorbed in helping Helen decide between a napoleon or gateau aux framboises. I realized then that I wanted much more than a glance from William and, at the same time, I knew it was impossible that more would be coming my way.

We said good night on the sidewalk in front of the restaurant and William put me in a taxi. As I waved good-bye out the back window, Helen took his arm and they began to walk back to their apartment.

Chapter 6

There was no time to brood over the next few weeks. I plunged into modeling with more fervor than I thought I had. I quickly became acquainted with the jargon of the business, which wasn't all that arcane, once you paid a little attention to it. A headsheet was just that, a sheet showing the heads of all the models an agency handled. A go-see was a similarly apt term. A model had to go and see a photographer so he could determine whether or not he wanted to use her for his shoot. A booker was the person who actually arranged—or booked—the assignments the model got, and as such was her most important connection. My booker at the Harold Ames Agency was Anita Weston, the rather plain girl who had acted as receptionist the first day I went there. She was pleasant, polite, and initially remote; it took me a couple of weeks to realize that if I was going to get anywhere in the business, I'd better be on her good side. At about the time this fact was dawning on me, Harold Ames called me in for a little talk.

"You know," he said after greeting me and chatting for a few minutes in a seemingly rambling way that was actually honing in on his subject, "modeling is just a business like any other. You can have all the looks and the talent in the world, but if you don't promote them you won't get anywhere."

"Yes, I suppose so," I said warily, wondering where the conversation was leading.

"Now take you, for example," said Harold, dropping his regard to the left of my eyes. "You're a beautiful girl and you photograph like a house afire. You're intelligent and can take directions. On the surface there's absolutely no reason why you shouldn't make it."

"Thank you," I said dubiously.

"*But*," he continued with a rueful smile, "you could still fuck up, if you know what I mean."

"Actually, I don't," I said chillingly. My stomach went hollow with apprehension.

Harold smiled and lifted his hand placatingly. "Diane, I'm just trying to give you a few tips. Believe me, it's for the good of both of us if you pay attention."

I gave him a glacial stare; I was terrified he was going to tell me I had somehow failed.

"When you become a model you start a business. And like any business, you need to sell yourself. It isn't enough just to walk in and be beautiful—you've got to present yourself like a well-run organization. You've got to do the expected things like being on time, and being cooperative. I can't fault you on those. But in addition, you've got to do a lot of public relations work for yourself—be nice, in other words. Be friendly, get along with the photographers—and your booker. You get in bad with either one and you might as well cut your throat.

"Now I haven't had any complaints, but I did talk to the guy you worked with on the eyewash commercial, and he called you the 'Ice Queen.' "

I blushed.

"He admitted," Harold continued, "that you had worked well, but he found you standoffish and snobbish. What was the problem?"

"I didn't think there was one. I was nervous, I guess." Then, more aggressively, I added, "What was I supposed to do? Make a pass at him?"

"Better not," said Harold drily. "He's gay, and wouldn't appreciate it. Just be friendly. You don't have to screw the photographers to get ahead—though it doesn't hurt. Just be human with them. Show an interest in the work, in *their* work, in the product—sell yourself." He raised his hands, palms upwards to signify how simple it was. "And about Anita. Be *very* nice to Anita. She's your booker, and she's going to work more closely with you than anyone else in the business, at least while you're with this agency. Get to know her. Take her out for a drink or dinner. Believe me, it's to your advantage. What did you do before you came here?"

"I was a bartender," I said defensively.

"Great! You must have had to soothe a lot of ruffled feelings and be nice to a lot of people you didn't particularly like. Great practice for being a model. I mean it. Treat the people you meet as though they were customers in your bar."

He was doing me a favor, yet I still had trouble accepting criticism. I sat for an instant, wondering how to react, when he reached over and patted my hand and smiled in such a sympathetic way that my reserve melted. "I'm sorry, Harold," I said.

"Don't be sorry. You're doing a terrific job, and you're going to have a terrific career. You're one in a million, which is why I'm taking the trouble to smooth over a few rough spots. I've got all the faith in the world in you."

I was as susceptible to compliments as to criticism and I left his office glowing. I walked directly to Anita's office—where she had been moved as the firm had expanded and hired a full-time receptionist—and asked her if she was free for dinner that evening. She was both free and surprised. I took her to Oren and Aretsky, and we exchanged girlish confidences well into the night. I learned that she had had experiences in school similar to mine, only she had grown up plain. Being a booker was, I suppose, one way for her to get back at all those beautiful people who had ignored her. As a booker she wielded enormous power over them. We both got a little tipsy on wine, and when we parted, I felt genuinely fond of her. She liked me, too, because two days later she threw the Tuxedo Towel assignment my way.

Tuxedo Towel was my first big breakthrough. It was a national print campaign that would run in every magazine in the country. I went on the go-see with my fingers crossed and my heart in my mouth. The photographer was Raymond Horn, one of the best-known in the business, and his studio was on Central Park South, twenty floors above the sound and soot of New York City. A whole wall of glass framed the undulating verdant rectangle that was Central Park.

There were people all over his reception room: models on go-sees for other jobs, assistants, fashion editors and one willowy secretary who kept us all in line. I was intimidated by the time she finally said to me, "Ray will see you now. You have your portfolio?"

I nodded and got up. She led me to a door set into a frame of glass bricks and opened it without knocking. "Here's Diane," she announced briskly and stepped aside.

Raymond Horn was sprawled on a rattan chaise longue, the sort you see in movies set in Rangoon. He was wearing tight Levis, sneakers and a stained white tee shirt through which I could see the outlines of a well-muscled body. His blond hair was fine and thin on top, thicker around the sides, and bristling into a formidable mustache under his nose. Bright blue eyes were startling against his deep tan and when he spoke his teeth gleamed like keys on a new piano.

"Hi," he said, shuffling a pile of prints on a table beside him. "Excuse the mess." He looked at me more closely and added, "I've been shooting a fashion layout all morning. You're a welcome change. It's good to see someone with tits." He laughed and swung upright on the settee.

If that remark had been made by a customer in my bar he would have been asked to leave; but I had been a model long enough to realize that references to my anatomy were not to be taken personally. Raymond Horn's allusion to my tits was comparable to a car dealer's comments on chrome trimming—it was just a passing observation, tinged, in this case, with admiration. I smiled with my newly acquired, if ersatz, assurance, and breezily returned his "Hi."

"Let's see your book," he said.

I gave him my portfolio, which was still thin, and he leafed through it in a few seconds while nodding. "You're pretty new." A statement, not a question.

"Fairly."

"I haven't seen you around." He looked at me with what seemed a mixture of professional and personal interest. "Not in ads and not in the flesh. Where do you hang out?"

"Oh, here and there. Nowhere much." I wasn't being coy. I really hadn't been going out since I had moved to New York. "I've only been here a few weeks."

"A few weeks?" He looked impressed and tapped my portfolio as he added, "And you've already had a couple of jobs? That's pretty good."

"Just lucky."

"Luck helps." He studied me. Then, he said decisively, "OK. You understand the layout?"

"No."

"It's for Tuxedo Towels. The model will have to be wet a lot, and she'll be draped in a sheet towel or maybe a couple of bath towels. And nothing else. That OK with you?"

"Sure," I said, not at all sure. After a pause I asked, "You mean, these'll be nude photographs?"

"No, sweetheart. *Good Housekeeping* and

Ladies' Home Journal don't go for nudes. Your nakedness will be disguised by yards of fluffy Tuxedo Towels. Underneath them, though, you will be bare. Are you up to that?"

"Sure."

He cocked an eyebrow and said, "I think you're going to work out." The statement was padded with innuendo.

"Great," I said, with the bounce of a cheerleader.

"I'll call your agency and book the time. It should be in two or three days." He stood up, and I saw he was not quite as tall as I, but his body was lean and compact. He reached for my hand across the cluttered coffee table and pressed it as he gave a crooked smile. "I'll see you."

"Thanks. And good-bye." I picked up my book and waved as I stepped back into the glass-walled reception room. I felt a flutter, as though I had been asked for a date by the captain of the football team. Raymond Horn's parting look promised a lot more than another job.

I was ready for him. While in Connecticut, I had discreet but regular—if not very exciting—sex. Since I had come to New York, I had not even had a drink with a man alone, much less gone to bed with one. There had been my stint watching Barry Boston perform with Cissie, and my dinner with William and his wife, and that was it. I was more than eager for whatever Raymond Horn had in mind.

My appetite was whetted by a comment that Anita made after Raymond's secretary had confirmed the booking. "So, you'll be working with Raymond Horn." She raised her eyebrows and smiled rather archly. "He's been known to take advantage of a girl."

"I guess I'll have to be on my guard," I said with wholesome jocularity, as every pore of my body anticipated the appointment.

Four days later, when I arrived at his studio a quarter of an hour before nine (Harold had counseled me always to be early), I was afraid that I had indulged in a pipe dream because it was filled with people. In my fantasies about my session with Raymond, there had been only him and me; I knew that was impossible, but I hadn't counted on the hordes I found there: make-up man, hairdresser, account executives, assistants and representatives from the client. There were at least fifteen people milling around, drinking coffee from Styrofoam cups and eating Danish. I checked in with the secretary and she called over the make-up man, a short black guy with a goatee and a head as smooth as an egg.

"This is Don," she said, and introduced me.

"Hi ya," he said. "Want some coffee?"

"No thanks." I looked around, hoping to see Raymond, but he was nowhere in sight. "What do I do now?"

"You get out of those clothes and get up on my little seat over there, and I'll put your make-up on." Don pointed to a small dressing room and at the same time held up a white cotton wrap-around. I was out of my jeans and sweater in a few minutes and perched on the high chair facing a light-encircled mirror.

"Now Ray doesn't want anything too fancy," said Don as he studied my face, "but I think I'll just play up those eyes a little, and bring out the cheekbones."

"OK." I was compliant, passive.

"You gotta be waterproofed because you're going to be soaked. You know that?"

"Yeah. I know I'll probably be wearing only a towel."

"Yep." He began to apply a base, not only to my face but also to my shoulders, neck and breasts. He covered the latter with as much disinterest as the former, dabbing with quick strokes to spread the cosmetic evenly. Self-consciously I looked through the open door while holding the wrap-around as close as possible, but no one paid any attention to me. The assistants were arranging lights, and the others were talking among themselves. The hairdresser, a stout woman in her thirties named Maureen, came by and fingered my hair, but otherwise I could have sashayed around the place completely nude, I felt, and be overlooked. I began to feel more at ease.

When Don finished, Maureen took over and put my hair up in cloth rollers, and after holding a hand drier to my head she combed me out. One of Raymond's assistants came by and, without greeting me, said to Don, "We're going to be doing her hands. Her nails look a little ragged." Don grimaced and said, "Shit." Then he said to the assistant, "I'll *try* to get a manicurist, but you *knew* you were going to do the hands when you called, and this shouldn't be my job."

The assistant shrugged and walked away as he said, "Ray's gonna be mad if her hands aren't done."

"That's no skin off my ass," said Don under his breath, but went to the phone and after a series of calls returned to say a manicurist was on the way. Half an hour later a thin, nervous black-haired girl arrived with her case and did my nails.

By then it was almost noon, and still no sign of Raymond. Another of his assistants came around asking us what we wanted for lunch, which he was going to order from the delicatassen.

As my tuna salad and coffee arrived so did Raymond Horn. He waved to all of us—a band of leaderless players—and disappeared into his office without greeting anyone in particular. I felt hurt; I had been looking forward all morning to that moment when our eyes would meet and though I knew nothing would be said, I was sure some signal would pass between us. A little later, when he emerged, he walked directly to the shooting area to inspect the setup, then came to where I was standing. He glanced expertly over me and said to Don, "There's too much around the eyes. Too made-up. We want a cross between a nice mommy and a homecoming queen. No glamour." He walked away. I might have been a brick wall.

As soon as Raymond left, Don muttered under his breath, but toned down the eyes and also retouched the rest of the make-up which had been marred by the hairdresser and lunch.

It was one o'clock, and suddenly, Raymond galvanized all of us by yelling, "Let's get going, everybody, we've got to wrap this up today. Got a lot to do." He had the back and umbrella lights switched on and then called to me in the same tone he had used with his assistants: "Diane, come over here and stand right in the center."

I was miffed; I walked to the photographic area in a fog of hostility. The backdrop and floor had been covered by a pink shiny oilcloth. Standing in the center with lights glowing on me from four directions, I felt as though I were in the middle of a rose. Pink has always been my favorite color, as well as my most flattering, so I began to feel somewhat soothed.

Raymond was looking at me through the sights of the test Polaroid. "Give her the pink towel," he said to an assistant, and a boy came over to me holding out a huge towel sheet. He nonchalantly removed my cotton wrap as I quickly pulled the towel around my shoulders.

"Not that way," said Raymond brusquely. "Under your arms and just over the tits. Like a sarong. You know what a sarong is?"

"Yes," I said icily. Then, remembering Harold's admonition to keep smiling, even if it was at an asshole, I blithely added, "Like in *The Blue Lagoon*."

"You got it," he said abstractedly, as I rearranged the towel. It was luxuriously soft and draped from my breasts to the floor in velvetlike folds.

"That's right," said Raymond, still crouched over his tripodded camera. "Hold it." The strobe flashed. I regained my composure as I told myself that it was, after all, a job, and I had been foolish to expect anything more. I had been guilty of romanticizing a mild flirtation, probably because I was just a wee bit horny. ("Horny for Horn," kept dancing through my head like a jingle.) I determined to get through the rest of the shoot with cheerful professionalism, and to forget whatever expectations had been built by Raymond's come-on several days before.

The test photograph showed the need for minor adjustments in the lights which were made, and the shooting began. Raymond started slowly, talking me from one pose to another.

"Bend back a little and look away. Lower the head, let your hair fall forward. That's right. Crook your knee. Show some leg, stick it out there. That's right." He never had any intention of using these initial shots. They were made to loosen me up and get me into the right mood for the pictures he wanted. I did begin to feel more relaxed and confident, and lost my hostility. I found myself listening to his voice, but watching the camera.

"Pout a little—not too much. Good. Now twirl. Make the hair fly. Again. Again. Good." I whirled and whirled and dizzily sought out the lenses. "Bend way over, mess up the hair. Now throw your head back. Good. Gimme your right shoulder. Thrust it way out. Raise your head. Smile. Just a little. Good." He called to one of his assistants, "Get her wet—not too much. Face, shoulders and tits."

The boy came over with a Windex bottle filled with water, and carefully sprayed me. Raymond took another camera and said, "You just got out of the shower. You feel great. You love that towel.

Ohhh, how you *love* that towel. Good." I did love the towel—it felt like a caress, and the sensation of it against my skin, linked with Raymond's voice, the warmth and the ever-prodding lenses of his Nikon was making my nipples hard.

The next two hours were a blur of commands, pink-hot lights, misted water, furry toweling against my skin, and a camera that in my imagination had grown a large burnished blond mustache; Raymond became inseparable from his Nikon.

The session flowed. I know, now that I have been on the other side of the camera, how rare and priceless that phenomenon is, when a model and photographer begin to anticipate each other. At the time I took it for granted that my response to the lens, after an hour or so, was normal. It was not—it was extraordinary, and the reason for my success. It was as though the lens was touching me physically, gently moving me from place to place, searching out feelings and shadows and undiscovered beauties. I came alive in a way I had never been alive before; I glowed. I was incandescent.

Excitement crackled between Raymond, Nikon and me. "Wet the lips a little, just a little, run your hand through your hair, up the back, keep it there. Right." He would stop to exchange his camera for a newly loaded one, and occasionally have Don retouch my make-up or Maureen comb out my hair, or the assistant spray me from the Windex bottle—pauses I resented, for I could hardly wait to dive back into the rapport that shimmered like a lake between us.

Finally the session came to a close. I was both

disappointed and exhausted. Raymond was drenched in sweat: beads of it ran in rivulets down his face and soaked his tee shirt, which clung to his chest and outlined his nipples. He looked triumphant, and was not even bothered when the account executive—a heavy, self-important man—worriedly said to him, "Some of that work looked a little . . . ah . . . almost raunchy to me."

"Don't panic," said Raymond, wiping his head with a Tuxedo Towel, "the print we use will make it look like only virgins, young marrieds, nuns and possibly the Queen Mother of England use Tuxedo Towels."

"Heh, heh," said the executive, not amused.

"I know the markets for the ad," said Raymond. "You'll get the right picture." He turned from the man in a much more cavalier way than most photographers would have treated a client. The executive, looking sour, left.

Don and Maureen said good-bye, and some of the assistants drifted off. I rested on a low stool, the towel still draped around me, feeling drained and let down, as though I had been discoing for several hours straight. Finally I pulled myself together and started toward the changing room when Raymond called, "Hey, Diane, where's your voucher?" He looked at me levelly with a silent smile.

"I have it in my purse. I'll fill it out right away." The voucher was like a time card that has to be filled out for each assignment.

I rummaged around in my purse a moment, annoyed, then turned to find Raymond standing in the doorway, smiling at me. "You lose it?" he asked, cocking an eyebrow.

I knew something was going on, but didn't understand what. "I couldn't have," I said. "It was here . . ."

Raymond took the purse and put it on the chair, then put his arms around me. "Why don't we relax a minute. It'll turn up."

We went back to the studio, where only two assistants were left. Raymond looked at them coldly and, though he said nothing, they understood enough to get out, keeping their expressions noncommittal. Raymond and I were alone.

"Well," he said. "Great session."

"Yeah."

"It's kinda hard to unwind after that. Maybe you'd join me in a little glass of wine?"

"Sure."

"Champagne, OK?"

"Domestic or imported?"

He laughed. "How about Mumms?"

"I can drink Mumms." I stood, still wearing the pink towel, my hair tousled, and looked directly in his eyes. We were both smiling slightly.

He took my hand and led me behind the studio into his apartment—a large, surprisingly conventional living room with overstuffed sofas and chairs and blow-ups of photographs on the walls. I sat on one of the sofas, and Raymond disappeared into the kitchen. He returned with two crystal goblets and a bottle of napkin-draped champagne. Carefully he began to work the cork out, until there was a small pop, and smoke rose from the neck. He poured and passed the wine as the bubbles streamed to the top and erupted on the surface.

We clicked glasses. "Here's looking at you," he said, then added, "sorry I can't come up with anything original. But it's the truth. I really am looking at you."

I sipped and smiled.

"We've been working like a couple of plow horses," he said. "We're all covered with sweat." He ran a finger lightly across my shoulder and down my arm. As he leaned closer, I inhaled the scent of his body.

"Plow horses!" I laughed. "Where're you from?"

"Minnesota. A farm in Minnesota. I know how a plow horse works." His fingers now ran up my arm, across my shoulder to my throat. He tickled the hollow of my throat until I lowered my chin and trapped his finger.

"Maybe," he continued, "we should wash off the day's dirt."

"Not a bad idea." I was pleased with myself. In only a few short weeks I was in a well-known photographer's living room, having—as I supposed—an affair. I thought back to my first night in the city, when I watched Barry Boston and Cissie like some little match girl staring through the window of a candy store. I laughed.

"What's the matter?"

"Nothing's the matter," I said, holding out my glass.

He poured more champagne, then got to his feet and pulled me after him. "Bring it with you," he said softly as he led me down a hall to the door at the end.

Raymond Horn's bathroom was the center of his social life. It was almost as big as the reception room and, like the reception room, one wall was sheer glass framing Central Park. Near the window, almost touching it, was a bathtub big enough for four people, set into a brownish-grey marble slab that was raised about two feet above the level of the floor, which was carpeted in white shag. As Raymond turned on the faucets, I looked at myself in the mirror that covered the upper part of one wall, above a counter of the same veined marble in which two sinks were set. I was flushed and my eyes were bright. Behind me Raymond was taking off his shirt. There was nothing so crude as a toilet in sight. As though he sensed my need, Raymond said, "The john's through there," and pointed to a door on the opposite wall, next to an oversized beige couch.

I went into the room which had not only toilet, but also shower and bidet—all streamlined and as conventional as anything you'd find in Connecticut.

When I returned, Raymond was naked and sitting on the edge of the tub with his back to me, his feet dangling over the side. He faced the huge window.

"Aren't you afraid your neighbors will call the police if you sit in front of the window that way?" I said, teasing.

"Any neighbors who see what goes on in this room, see it through a telescope. If they complain, I'll have them arrested for peeping." He smiled up at me, and added, "Is that towel stuck to you?"

"I think I can pry it off." I loosened the fold over my breasts and let the towel fall in a downy pink heap to the marble.

Raymond looked. I didn't feel self-conscious standing in front of the whole upper part of Manhattan without a stitch. Through the glass wall, the mammoth apartment houses that ringed the park sparkled from thousands of windows and the park itself glowed green, as moving headlights snaked through the roadways. We were in the center of millions of people, and as remote as if we'd been on a space ship.

Raymond took my hand and pulled me gently to the edge of the tub. I tested the water with my toes, then eased my legs into it as I sat next to him. He slipped off the side and submerged himself up to his neck, then grabbed my foot and tugged. I laughed and glided into the warm bath. We stretched out side by side, barely touching; our feet would brush, or our thighs or arms. We lay for a few moments and relaxed as I looked at the night sky illuminated by New York below.

Raymond fingered my neck, ribs, waist and back; he didn't touch my breasts or pussy. I responded by caressing his shoulders, which were muscled and hard, and his firm sides and waist. I, too, shied away from his more sensitive areas. It became a game with us to find and explore our non-erogenous zones, which thereby became erogenous.

After fifteen minutes I was as limp as a strand of spaghetti, and I floated passively into Raymond's plans, whatever they might be. He pulled me to my feet and we soaped each other with a pink jar that smelled like raspberries. It was my first view of him standing nude.

I was surprised at how small his cock was. Now I think that his mustache—so thick and luxuriant—had led me to expect a huge cock. I don't know why I should have associated the two, but I did. On another man, Raymond's cock might have been a disappointment, but he wore it with such panache that I hardly noticed it was smaller than average, and backed by a small scrotum; also, it was covered by a foreskin, which was then a novelty to me, and gave it an appealing mystery, as though it were wearing a disguise. His pubic hair was golden and thick in the white hand that appeared sprayed across his belly where his swimsuit had protected his skin from turning as mahogany as the rest of him. The sun had bleached the fine curling hairs on his upper chest, so that they were platinum against the foil of his tan. His body was hard and defined, though not exaggeratedly muscled.

As we lathered, Raymond still avoided touching my breasts and pussy, and I soaped those areas myself; I reciprocated by avoiding his cock and nipples. We submerged and rinsed, and then stepped out of the tub. From a folded pile, Raymond pulled a large white sheet towel, draped it around me and patted me dry, then used the same towel for himself.

We hardly talked at all. Our movements were languorous, oiled into effortlessness by the champagne, which we carried to the huge couch facing the mirror.

I sank into the pillows and stretched, pulling my arms over my head and extending my toes as far as they would go. Raymond stood over me, and brushed the hair back from my forehead, then kissed my eyes with soft lips as his still-damp mustache brushed over my face like a mist. He lifted my feet to the couch, turning me so that I could lie back on the velvet pillows. Leaning on his arms, he bent over and kissed me; his tongue darted into my mouth and across my teeth and out again, then he ran it over the edge of my lips. I tried to contact it with my own tongue but he was too quick. I put my arms around his neck, and smoothed his shoulders with my palms.

Raymond straddled but did not touch my waist; he carefully removed my hands from his body and placed them over my head, as though I were being held up.

"Just lie there," he whispered.

He moved back until he was kneeling over my feet, then lowered his face to my calf and blew on it before licking it with darting stabs. Blowing and licking he progressed to my inner thigh, leaving a trail of sensations so subtle they seemed imagined. He approached my pussy, and his tongue sought out the smooth hairless joints on either side of it where my thighs merge with my body. He licked and lightly bit each cleft, then supporting himself on his arms, hovered over my pussy as I anticipated the moment he would touch—simply touch—it. He did not touch it, but lowered his face to my belly button and worked lightly around it with his tongue.

Slowly he moved upward until he reached my breasts and blew on the nipples, first the left then the right, but did not touch them, then his tongue traced a line down my cleavage, on down to the belly button and farther to my pussy, where he blew in little puffs, then passed over it again to nip my inner thigh.

I squirmed and moaned. My anticipation of the moment he would touch me became a tangible part of the pleasure I was feeling as I lay, my arms stretched above, watching Raymond's head through the valley of my breasts. He bobbed over my pussy and I felt his breath; so delicately I would not have been sure if I hadn't been watching, his tongue outlined my labia. I could not help thrusting upward, trying to lure the tongue deeper into my pussy, but he, suspended on his arms, raised his head and flowed up my belly to my breasts. He blew on the nipples again, then touched one, then the other, then lightly closed his mouth around the left one. I was so hot that I moaned as though he had shoved his cock into me. He moved from the left to the right nipple and back again until they were both so tender that my shoulders curled inward when he took one or the other between his lips.

He ran his tongue down my abdomen, and used it to nudge between the lips of my pussy. My legs spread wider as he delicately probed. He found my clitoris and lingered there, gently massaging it. I burst into my first orgasm.

I had five orgasms over the next hour; they were like small explosions of Chinese firecrackers, each detonation strung to the last. Raymond continued to glide from nipple to pussy, with maverick caresses to points between and below. He sucked more and more forcibly on my breasts, and finally buried his face in my pussy while his tongue delved deeper and deeper. My whole body tingled; it was a nation and my pussy was its capital, governing its extremities.

My last orgasm caused me to scream, something I never did back in Connecticut, and I moaned with relief as I sank into the cushions, and Raymond stretched out beside me. I wanted him to share my pleasure, and I reached for his cock. He kept my hand away from it, though, and began to masturbate himself while holding his mouth over my breast. Almost immediately he moaned and shot sperm onto my abdomen, then he dropped his head on my shoulder.

We lay, our arms around each other, for a long time. I felt slight, almost incorporeal. We dozed for a little while—no more than fifteen or so minutes—then, with a smiling sigh, Raymond knelt on the floor, took my hand between his hands and kissed me on the lips.

"You have the most incredible cunt," he said.

It was not quite the romantic statement I would have preferred, but I was pleased enough to laugh. "Thanks," I said, while groping for some reciprocal compliment. All I could think of was praise for his mouth, but I held back.

The champagne was warm and flat, but it tasted delicious just the same as we finished the few sips in the bottle. I went into the john and when I came out, Raymond had returned to the living room, though he was still naked. He smiled as I entered, then looked at the coffee table. There was a voucher I knew I had put in my purse before leaving.

"How did that get there?" I asked in mock wonder.

"I dunno. I'm glad you lost it though." He raised both eyebrows.

I fell to the couch facing him, and put my arms around his neck and my face close to his. "Thank you, Raymond . . . I've never . . . never . . ."

"You never knew it could be like this?" he asked with ironical good humor.

"Something like that."

He pulled me closer and we kissed. Our naked bodies fit each other so comfortably and felt so right, as though our union completed a jigsaw puzzle. I could have lingered for hours, but Raymond discouraged that notion after a few minutes by saying, "I've got to get up at six tomorrow. Going out on location."

I sighed. "Me too. I mean, I've got an early call." I put my hand on his face, then smoothed his mustache while sitting on his lap. "Will you sign my voucher now, so I can go?" I asked solemnly.

He smiled and reached around me for the piece of paper on the table, and held it before my eyes. It was filled in and signed.

I got up and went back to the studio where I dressed quickly. It seemed like weeks since I had taken my clothes off. Raymond, still naked, stood watching me.

When I was ready to leave I turned expectantly and he took me in his arms. "Thank you, Diane," he said.

"Thank you," I replied, kissing him. I added, "I hope we can see each other again."

"You bet." He smiled. "I'll call you soon."

As I left the studio, I waved to him standing in the crack of the open door. He waved back and shut the door and I heard the locks turn as the elevator arrived.

Chapter 7

On my bedroom wall there is a blow-up of the picture the Tuxedo Towel people chose for their campaign. I'm standing in the middle of a pink glow, wrapped in a pink towel, shaking out my hair and I look radiant, as though being wrapped in a Tuxedo Towel was the best thing that could ever happen to a girl. At the same time I am open, friendly, beautiful and *clean.* I don't think I've ever looked so clean. It's one of my favorite pictures from that first year.

On the evening William called, I glanced at it again in the light of the silently flickering TV screen, and thought back to that night with Raymond Horn. With a smile that was probably a little rueful, I realized how much I had changed. When I left Raymond's apartment I did not tell him I loved him—as I would have a few years earlier—but I was certain that at least I was going to see him again and, I hoped, often. I never did. Or rather, I never saw him in any way other than professionally. During the week following our lovemaking high above Central Park, I kept waiting for Raymond to call, or make some gesture (maybe, I though, he'd send flowers) or some acknowledgment of what had passed between us. Nothing. I became so depressed that Anita noticed and brought it to the attention of Harold. He had a talk with me—in a fatherly, worried way—but I didn't tell either of them that I was mooning over Raymond. I was hurt and lonely, but I kept the pain to myself, as I had learned to do years before as a young girl. At any rate, I emerged from the next few weeks with an even thicker carapace around my emotions—not a bad thing to have in this town in this business.

On the wall of my bedroom, next to the Tuxedo Towel picture is another picture of me, looking entirely different: hair swept up, expression serene and, around my neck, three strands of pearls. It was a head shot, cut off just above the breasts. And next to that is another photograph, of a gorilla in a cage at the Central Park Zoo, sitting in a tire, looking wearily through the bars directly at the lens. The two photographs are milestones of a sort in my life, and both explain why I was not devastated by Raymond Horn's fickleness.

The picture of me in pearls was taken by Arthur Mane, who, in his late sixties, was considered if not the dean of American photography, at least one of its most eminent elder statesmen. The necklace came from a famous jeweler who was also an arch patriot and born-again Christian, and who took an equal amount of newspaper space to expound his views on God and country as to peddle his baubles. This jeweler, Adolph Griffin, hired the best photographer he knew of for his advertising departure: the use of a live model. Before that, he, like most jewelers, simply photographed the jewelry. But he would not accept just any model; it had to be someone who was both beautiful and wholesome, yet sophisticated enough not to be eclipsed by thousands of dollars' worth of necklaces, brooches, earrings, and so on. By the time my portfolio was submitted, Adolph Griffin had reportedly vetoed over a hundred candidates, and the newspapers had taken up the story of the search for the "Griffin Girl!"

He did not veto me. Instead, he asked that I come by his office for an interview. I arrived, early, and was ushered in immediately to a large bare room above his store on Fifth Avenue. Mr. Griffin's office was more austere than Harold's at the agency: a wooden desk, highbacked chair, Oriental rug and wingback chair for visitors. There was nothing on the walls and nothing—not even a telephone—on the desk. Mr. Griffin was about seventy or so years old, thin, erect and chillingly polite. He looked at me, smiled, nodded, and said, "Yes, you'll do." The interview was over: I became the Griffin Girl. It was the only time I ever saw him.

I saw a lot of Arthur Mane. He was a painstaking photographer and, unlike the people I had worked with up to that point, was self-effacing and soft-spoken. He had achieved that degree of fame that almost demands an accompanying modesty. It's possible that in his younger days he had been more volatile; by the time I worked with him, however, he was unvaryingly calm. A session with Arthur Mane was unlike any other I've had before or since.

His studio was on upper Fifth Avenue—an unusual location—and was a small room in a relatively small apartment. I never saw more of the apartment than the foyer, and a glimpse down a short hall to a dark living room. I don't believe he had a view of the park. As soon as I arrived I was ushered directly into the studio by an elderly secretary who wore rimless glasses and had a pencil stuck into her hair. She tapped softly on the door to the studio, then opened it and said, "Miss Bourne is here, Arthur." I believe she was the only person in the world who called him Arthur; his wife was dead.

Arthur Mane was short and ascetically thin, with a fringe of wispy grey hair around a pinkish pate, and very black, youthful eyes that were misplaced in the wrinkles surrounding them. He was wearing a subdued striped tie but no jacket, dark trousers and shined shoes. He stood, took my hand and formally said, "How do you do, Miss Bourne?"

We chatted for a few moments about the weather, then the make-up man and hairdresser arrived—both men accustomed to working with Mr. Mane, and older than those I'd met before. At ten-thirty, two guards from Griffin entered, one of them carrying a small chest. They were tall, burly men, looking exactly what guards should look like, and wore guns in holsters around their waists. They looked at me a lot.

By that time I was wearing a wrap-around, my hair had been brushed up and sprayed into place and my face had been painted on. Mr. Mane courteously asked me to stand on the white paper roll that was hanging from the ceiling and pulled over the floor. He made a Polaroid test shot, adjusted the lights, made another shot, then another. Finally, he declared himself satisfied and the shoot began.

A stool was placed in the middle of the photographic area. From the chest of jewels came an emerald and diamond necklace with matching earrings. The necklace was cold against my skin. Mr. Mane had me sit on the stool as he arranged and rearranged the necklace, earrings and strands of hair; he had eyebrows painted a bit darker, eye shadow made a bit lighter, lips a little more glossy—all before ever once snapping a shot. Finally, he went back to his camera, which remained on a tripod for most of the session, and clicked the shutter. He had me move a fraction of an inch to the left, told me to look up just a little, to hold my head just slightly to the right; he readjusted the jewelry, and a strand or two of hair, issuing all requests in quiet conversational tones. When I was exactly as he wanted me, he clicked again.

In this slow, careful way he continued to work. There was none of the razzmatazz I had come to expect from photographers, no "Give me a smile!" or "Let's have a pout!" Instead, he molded me as meticulously as a sculptor, even down to having me extend my little finger just a millimeter to the left.

Yet working with him was never tedious. He was so sure of what he was doing that I didn't mind being a piece of raw material in his hands. I became so interested in his style, and in his general work (he had published several books of photographs that I looked at in a bookstore after the first day) that the shoot became a classroom for me. It took Mr. Mane a week to create the four pictures that Griffin finally used for the campaign; that week changed my life, because that is when I became interested in working on the other side of the camera.

My desire to become a photographer was not as spur of the moment as it might seem. I had long wanted to make something of my life, and just as an accidental introduction of a grain of sand into an oyster can eventually become a pearl, so a seemingly random encounter can grow into a career. Mr. Mane showed me what an artist could do, and impressed me with the possibilities of photography. I didn't dare, of course, to confide my sudden ambition to anyone, least of all to Mr. Mane. But I did buy a Leica, and began to attack the visual world around me. In my spare moments nothing was safe from my lens. I indiscriminately photographed children, animals, trees, flowers, buildings, cars and crowds—suddenly everything looked like a good picture. I talked to Mr. Mane whenever I could.

"Did it take you a long time to become a good photographer?" I asked him on the fourth day of our session.

He smiled. "I'm still working on it," he said.

"But how long do you think it should take someone to become a professional?"

He shrugged. "Overnight. All you need to do is buy a camera and push a button, and charge for the results."

"But a *good* professional?"

"That's something else. It depends."

"On what?" I persisted. I was so obviously sincere he wasn't annoyed; also, he was invariably polite.

"Well, there's technique, of course. Though

that's overrated. Eventually anyone can master technique. Then there's taste, and that's more difficult to come by. Not everyone has it. But I guess I'd say you become a good photographer when your technique catches up with your taste."

This was one of those oracular statements that makes the head spin at the time of pronouncement, but doesn't bear much weight upon closer scrutiny. It was both true and practically meaningless. I eventually learned that you become a good photographer when you start taking good photographs. It's as simple and complex as that. Another Delphic utterance.

Anyway, by the end of the week with Arthur Mane, I was emboldened enough to ask him if I could work with him in my spare time. He was astonished.

"I don't believe I quite understand you, Miss Bourne. What is it you want to do?"

"I want to learn to be a good photographer."

"Then take pictures."

"But I need help—guidance."

"I can't give you lessons."

"But you can let me work with you—as an assistant or something, can't you? Couldn't I just watch you work whenever I have the time? I wouldn't be in the way or be a nuisance."

He was perplexed and embarrassed. Of course, he didn't want a dilettante cluttering up his studio—already crowded because it was so small—yet I struck a responsive nerve. I wanted to learn from Arthur Mane so badly it hurt, and my pain must have shown in my plea.

"But you're a model. You have a full-time career."

"I'm not working every hour of the day, or even every day of the week. I have the time. I can make more. I know I don't have anything to offer in exchange, but I can promise that I'll never become a nuisance, never be in the way."

He sighed and looked at his watch. "We must finish the series today. Let me think about it."

It was the last day of the shoot, and I was to model the pearls—perfectly matched and almost priceless, a unique piece of jewelry. Mr. Mane molded me as scrupulously as for all the other shots, and at the end of the three hours had taken as many pictures. I didn't pursue my goal verbally, but I couldn't help watching him expectantly during the breaks in the session. I was possessed with the idea of working for him; I had never been so absolutely certain of what I wanted in my life.

At the end of the day he called me aside. "You are a beautiful girl, and an excellent model. You have a good career ahead of you. I have no idea whether you would be a good photographer or not. I can't encourage you. On the other hand, I can't discourage you, either, beyond pointing out that because you're a model, and because you're a girl and, yes, because you're so beautiful, you will run into difficulties and prejudices that would never happen to someone without those attributes."

"I don't care," I said.

He smiled. "Well, we'll just have to see. You can watch me for the next month, on the days and during the hours you're free. At the end of that time we'll know whether it'll work out or not."

So I began my apprenticeship to Arthur Mane.

I became obsessed with taking pictures. All my free time was consumed by the pursuit of photographs. Simultaneously, my career as a model was taking off, and I was, as they say, "hot." Within six months I was able to be choosy about bookings, and to turn down those which I thought might be boring. I survived my month trial with Arthur Mane, and he rather resignedly told me that if I still wished to, I could consider myself a sort of apprentice. What it meant was that I could watch him work, and occasionally help him when our schedules meshed. It was an incredibly kind and generous gesture, and I'll always be grateful. I tried to compensate in any way I could; I would even dash out for coffee and sandwiches for everyone if need be, but mostly I just padded around after Mr. Mane, snatching whatever crumbs he let drop.

After about three months I started bringing some of my own pictures for him to criticize. He would look them over carefully, politely, but would hardly ever comment beyond making a specific suggestion: "Your background is too busy here." Or, "There's a hot spot there." Then, after a year, I took a series of animal pictures at the Central Park Zoo. I knew they were better than anything else I'd ever done and I was particularly pleased with the shot of the gorilla who sat so resigned, bored and dignified.

Mr. Mane, as he always did, began to look through the prints, carefully examining each, and then putting them face up on the table. He got to the gorilla picture, smiled slightly, and said, "This is nice."

It was the first compliment he ever paid me. Tears came to my eyes, but did not spill over. I was unable to speak. We both continued to look at the picture for an instant, then he put it on the table and went through the rest.

"You're coming along," he said quietly. "I confess you're much better than I ever thought you'd be."

"Thank you."

"You might want to consider fashion. With your background and all. Perhaps you should start to get a book together—that is, if you're serious about going professional."

"I am."

He smiled, shuffled through the prints, paused at the one of the gorilla again, and nodded. It was one of the happiest days of my life.

I reaped another dividend from my apprenticeship, in addition to a new career. Between my bookings as a model and my working with Mr. Mane, I had almost no time for the social life that beguiles so many models: the late nights at discos, the dinners at "in" restaurants, the weekends in Puerto Rico and the Bahamas—all the glamorous perquisites that can go with success in the business. Lately I've had more time to observe that fringe of activity around successful models. I don't like the men much; so many of them derive their whole worth from having a beautiful girl on their arms. The girls thereby become willing objects, playthings.

It can't help but make them feel like expensive toys, and like toys, they can be discarded when a spoiled owner spots something else more fun to play with. With my ingrained lack of assurance, one or two affairs of that sort might have done me in. When there was not a word from Raymond Horn after my one night in his bathroom I had been despondent and shaken. I can imagine how much more devastated I would have been if he had seen me a couple of times, maybe taken me to dinner, and then dropped me.

I soon recovered from Raymond Horn's indifference and learned that sex can be—usually is—a casual pastime. Back in Connecticut, I had always managed to imbue each encounter with at least a veneer of friendship that might, if you didn't look too closely, pass for affection. I gave up that pretence after six months in New York. Though I never stopped searching for the emotional equivalent of a good fuck, I didn't let its lack deter me from physical satisfaction. In short, I became a native.

Chapter 8

Encouraged by Mr. Mane, I began to assemble a book of my work. I suppose my existence could have become schizophrenic—I was so engrossed by both modeling and photography, and so attentive to each, that I concentrated completely on whichever I happened to be working on at the moment. That is not to say, however, that I didn't cross-fertilize the careers. As a model, I learned from watching good photographers work with me, and as a photographer, I studied the tricks used by different models, and incorporated any I thought I could use.

Following the advice of Mr. Mane, I decided to break into fashion photography, so the work I began to assemble was along those lines. I did not yet have my own studio, so I had to borrow or rent space for my shoots. Also, I was highly suspect; both art directors and models thought I was just dabbling. It took a lot of persuasion on my part to get models to test with me, and then to get art directors to look at my work. But I persevered; in spite of my fragile self-esteem, I am extremely assertive—aggressive, even—when I set my mind on a goal. For the first time in my life, I was actively working for something I wanted—a career as a fashion photographer.

Finally, I got my first assignment. It was only a two-page spread on lingerie for *Mode* magazine, and like all such jobs it paid hardly at all, but was an invaluable credit, and would be a marvelous addition to my book. I rented a studio from a group of photographers on West Twenty-first Street, and put in a call to a model agency that handled fashion, who sent four of their girls on go-sees.

The two I chose were roommates: as it turned out, they were more than that. Both were dark, five foot eight and slender. Angela had brown hair and green eyes and a full sensual mouth. Rena's hair was black, her eyes were blue and she had a slight overbite which gave her face an interesting provocativeness. Their complexions were smooth and clear, and their breasts minimal; with her short hair, Angela looked almost boyish. Though both girls had been models longer than I, each was younger. Angela was twenty-two and Rena, twenty. They had begun work when they were fifteen.

I was nervous on the morning of the shoot and initially, the behavior of Angela and Rena did nothing to reassure me. Though on time, and punctiliously polite, they were wary and suspicious. They made little comments and jokes between themselves that excluded me, and I felt a barely disguised hostility. As always, when I'm uncomfortable, I became icily proper. The art director from *Mode,* a dowdy woman with messy greying hair, didn't help matters any by making some last minute changes in the layout. The atmosphere, as the make-up and hair was done on Angela and Rena, was tense. I had lathered myself into believing that the success of my whole life depended absolutely on the outcome of this shoot.

The concept was mostly mine. We would show the lingerie worn by two models in a fantasy setting. They would emerge from many-hued swirls of mist which I would create with colored lights and huge blocks of dry ice. I had hired an assistant—a boy named Frank who worked for one of the regular photographers in the studio I was renting—in order to help me lug around the tubs of water in which the ice was placed in order to make it smoke, and to keep an eye out to make sure the flashes went off. Other than him, I was on my own.

I got the first shot set up. Three tubs of water were bubbling away, sending thick clouds into the air. Frank and I had positioned blue and red spots, and we tried the fan at various speeds to get the draft that would thin the vapors but not completely dissipate it. We were ready for the models, and I turned to them.

They had been standing to one side watching me drag the heavy tubs, cart the dry ice, wrestle with the lights, and they seemed snootily amused, as though they were gentry come to watch the peasants plow. I was sweaty and nervous, and in no mood to be condescended to.

"Please stand over here," I said, without a glimmer of friendliness, indicating the center of the shooting area, between two of the tubs.

Angela raised her eyebrows as both sashayed to the spot indicated. Angela was in a blue bra and panties, and Rena was wearing a pink camisole with ruffles along top and bottom.

They stood where I told them to and looked at me, I thought rather defiantly.

"OK, Angela," I said briskly, "stand about three-quarters facing me with your back to Rena. Rena, you look up, over Angela's shoulder. Angela, look off into the distance . . . no, not like that. Look as though you wondered where you were. . . ." They were both such pros that they instantly fell into my directions. What I wanted, and what I got from them, was a kind of innocent wonderment, as though they were two Alices who had fallen down some rabbit hole. The contrast between the scanty lingerie and their supposed naiveté was what was going to create the tension that would make the layout more, I hoped, than just a preview of the season's new undies.

We had to work very fast because, as the *Mode* art director kept reminding me, "We don't have any budget for overtime on this." I rushed everyone—Angela and Rena, the make-up woman (whom I had hired to do both hair and make-up because I'd noticed that one person in charge of both was not only cheaper in the long run, but also worked faster), Frank and myself. I even curtailed the time for lunch, which usually was a sacrosanct hour, by urging everyone back to work a good fifteen minutes early. I risked fanning a revolt, but this was my first assignment, and not only did it have to be perfect, it also had to be done on time and under budget.

As we worked into the afternoon and I realized that I was going to complete the shoot on schedule, and maybe a little sooner, I relaxed. I also perceived that after what I had considered their initial snottiness, Angela and Rena had thrown themselves into the session with gratifying gusto. They were terrifically good models, not only interestingly beautiful, but also capable of assuming instantly any pose I demanded. The shoot would never have gone so smoothly, and certainly not with such good results, had it not been for their cooperation. Their attitude toward me had remained distant—as had mine toward them—but at their work they were consummate pros. I felt a wave of gratitude for both about four o'clock as I was getting the last shot set up. Frank and I lugged those damned tubs around some more, and placed the lights, then I called, with more warmth than I had allowed myself before, "OK, girls, we're ready for you."

As they walked toward the shooting area I smiled and said, "This is the last one. You've both been terrific. Thanks a lot."

"All in a day's work," said Angela airily, but with a theretofore unaccustomed hint of friendliness. Rena, more shy, smiled charmingly.

For the last picture I had Angela, in a pink strapless bra, fastening Rena's white lace bra as both looked like children lost in a purple mist that obscured them from the waist down. They continued to give me the exact poses I wanted, and kept their expressions alive and involved.

"That's it," I said triumphantly, as I clicked my last shot at exactly four forty-five. I had completed my assignment fifteen minutes under schedule and, what was more, I was certain it was good work. I walked to the two girls who stood smiling in the middle of the dry-ice vapor and put my hand on a shoulder of each. "That does it. Thanks a million. You've been just great."

"So've you," said Angela without a trace of her smartaleckness. "It's been fun."

Unnecessarily, I said, "This is my first shoot." Then I blushed as though I'd revealed my innermost secret.

"No shit?" said Angela without sarcasm. "Well, you sure did a bangup job. Didn't she?" She turned to Rena.

"Terrific," said Rena shyly.

"Maybe," Angela began, hesitated, then more boldly continued, "maybe we ought to have a drink to celebrate. Can we buy you a drink?"

The editors from *Mode* were scurrying away, and I hardly knew Frank. I was high with satisfaction and tension, and I didn't want to be alone, so I said, "You sure can. Just as soon as you're ready to go." We all giggled a little, just from the excitement of the moment, and Angela and Rena went to change into their street clothes while I gave the film to Frank to take to the lab to be developed.

In a few minutes Angela and Rena came out of the dressing room in blue jeans and bulky sweaters, with scarves on their heads. Like most models going to or from an assignment, they looked rather frumpy. I was no fashion plate myself, for that matter, for I had worked the whole day in white coveralls and sneakers, my hair pulled back in a ponytail.

We were suddenly timid with each other, now that we were switching from a business to a social sphere, and our conversation in the elevator going down was strained and giggly. We walked out onto Twenty-first Street and we might as well have been in the middle of Des Moines at midnight for all the opportunities for sociability that presented themselves. We peered doubtfully up and down the street, then Angela said, "Look, this is creepy. Why don't we just grab a cab and go to our place?"

"I don't want to put you to any trouble," I said.

"It's less trouble than bopping around down there looking for a bar. Come on, we can take our shoes off and be comfortable." Without waiting for an answer she yelled "Taxi!" at a passing Checker. Angela was very much a take-charge type of person.

I was surprised when she gave the driver an address on Park Avenue in the Seventies, and even more surprised when we pulled up to one of those huge solid luxury buildings that seemed to have been created to house old-money families. A doorman in a forest-green uniform with gold trimming opened the cab door and deferentially greeted Angela and Rena, and nodded quite humbly to me. My soiled white coveralls seemed inadequate to the occasion as we walked down a marble and crystal hallway to a waiting elevator, where another uniformed attendant was waiting to waft us to the sixth floor. The elevator opened to a small foyer for Angela's and Rena's apartment.

The apartment had been part of a duplex which had been divided some years back. The living room was enormous, and carpeted in light blue. There were two art nouveaulike white overstuffed couches flanking the fireplace, tables with mirror tops and huge sprays of fresh roses, gladioli and daisies everywhere.

"How nice," I said inadequately, as I looked around.

"Oh, it's a dump, but it's home," said Angela with a campy wave of her hand. "Have a seat and tell us what you want to drink."

"White wine, if you have it . . ."

"Sure." She and Rena disappeared and returned a few minutes later with a tray and glasses, and minus their bulky sweaters. They took off their shoes and curled up on either end of the couch facing me. Angela opened a lapis lazuli box on the end table and took out a plastic sack and small sheaf of rice papers. She casually rolled a joint, lit it and passed it to me. When I declined, she gave no sign of caring one way or the other and held it to Rena, who inhaled deeply with a whoosh, then assumed that meditative and constipated look of all pot smokers holding their breath.

Angela raised her glass and said, "Here's to Diane on the success of her first shoot." Rena leaned forward and clinked glasses, then both turned to me.

"Thanks," I said, embarrassed and pleased. "It's so great of you to have me up to celebrate."

"It's great to have a non-paying guest," said Angela and giggled. Rena looked at her with mild reproach.

I didn't understand the allusion, so I just smiled pleasantly, with my best Connecticut manners.

"Well, what's next on your agenda?" asked Angela.

"I've got some bookings next week to model, but nothing yet to photograph. It's been pretty hard breaking into photography—if one assignment means I've broken in, that is."

Angela looked reflective as she sucked on the joint. Then, in the strained voice of someone holding her breath, she said, "Maybe we could help there." She passed the joint to Rena.

"Oh?" I said politely.

"Yeah." Angela expelled what little smoke she hadn't absorbed. "We've got a friend who sometimes needs some special photography. . . ." She looked at Rena. "Mark."

"Um," said Rena doubtfully, and glanced at me.

"Well," I said brightly, "anything you know of I'd appreciate hearing about."

"I'll call him later," said Angela.

There was an awkward silence, and to break it I seized upon the apartment again. "This is really a beautiful room. You're so lucky to find it in such a good neighborhood."

"Luck had nothing to do with it," said Angela, giggling "We worked our asses off to get it. Literally." She giggled again and looked at Rena, who smiled before sliding her eyes toward me to judge my reaction.

I smiled pleasantly. "I guess you've been very successful. That's understandable, because you're both so good."

Both Angela and Rena laughed. "Well," said

Angela, "that's truer than you know. We *are* good. Aren't we?" She patted Rena affectionately on the knee. "But," she continued goodhumoredly, "we have to work very hard. Like we did a couple of nights ago." Both giggled. Then Angela looked at me and said, "Don't mind us. We're just a little hysterical. We had a gig a few nights ago that just about knocked us flat."

"Really?" I said. I was beginning to feel out of place, and wondering how soon I could gracefully leave.

As though she sensed my discomfort, Angela said, "Excuse us, Diane. We're so silly because we're just winding down, not only from your shoot but from a job we had the night before."

"Oh, don't apologize." In my most proper voice I added, "I know how much a strain certain jobs can be."

This set them off again. They both giggled while I, feeling foolish and annoyed, kept a set smile on my face.

"We're going to have to tell you what happened or you're going to think we're off our rockers," said Angela, trying to be serious. "It's just that it was so goddamned funny." She asked Rena, "You don't really mind, do you?"

Rena shrugged, the pot and wine having evidently weakened her inhibitions.

"Well, look," said Angela to me, "Rena and me, we, well, we turn a few tricks for cash, you know what I mean? That's how we can afford this apartment."

I made sure to keep my expression noncommittal. Actually, I didn't care if they peddled their asses, or anything else, for that matter, but I'm conventional enough to have certain stock reactions, and when someone announces she's a prostitute my facial muscles automatically wanted to pinch into disapproval. "Oh, really," I said pleasantly.

"Yeah, and the other night we had this john . . ." she began to giggle, "this john you wouldn't believe."

"I guess . . ." I began, at a loss; then I plunged ahead, "I guess you can run into a lot of strange people that way." My remark surely took the prize for inanity.

"Weird," agreed Angela, "but what was really funny about him was that he thought he was so . . . so with it." She laughed again, and got to her feet. "He walked into the room like Mr. Macho—not a bad-looking guy really. Tall, a little paunch, but nothing serious, and a kind of reddish face—about forty, I'd say. Anyway, he came walking across the room," and here Angela threw back her shoulders, stuck out her pelvis and took long, lumbering strides toward the sofa, ". . . like King Kong off his leash. And he said, 'Sure am glad to meet yew gals.' We knew he was from Texas—they'd told us that when they called to make the appointment for him—but what we didn't know was that he'd *sound* and *look* like he was from Texas. . . ."

Rena interrupted. "Actually, he had kinda mean-looking little eyes."

"Well, yeah, I suppose, but on the whole, he wasn't bad. We've seen worse."

"That's true." Rena shrugged, and took another hit on the joint.

"So, anyway," continued Angela, "he comes in and plops down," she fell back on the couch, her legs thrown wide, her chest stuck out and her hands behind her head, "and you know what the first thing he says is? He says 'Waal, now, how'd a coupla nice chicks like you get into this business?' I couldn't *believe* it."

"Did you ever hear anything so tacky?" asked Rena.

"It certainly was tactless," I said judiciously. I was wondering the same thing myself. I was at a loss as to how to react; both the girls were high on pot and wine and were, I was afraid, telling me things they'd regret when they sobered up. I felt uneasy, like an accidental eavesdropper. Angela and Rena, however, seemed as unconcerned as if they were reciting a grocery list.

"Tactless is about the nicest thing you could say about him," continued Angela. "We were sitting on either side of him and he put his arms around each of our necks and pulled us closer—in a strangle hold—and said, 'I just want yew girls to know that anything goes with ole Billy Ray.' Billy Ray was his name. Then he unzipped his fly and took out his cock and balls, and said, 'Now what you two think of that?' " Angela rolled her eyes to the ceiling, and Rena giggled, shaking her head.

I felt called upon to say something. "Uh . . . was it nice?"

"The cock?" asked Angela and shrugged. "It was big. I guess it was OK if you like cocks. I don't have much use for them myself." She patted Rena on the knee, and they smiled at each other; I smiled too, constrainedly. "Anyway," said Angela, "there he lolled, squeezing our necks, with his cock hanging outside his pants. He pushed my head down to it and said, 'Kiss it, sweetheart.' I took it in my mouth—that's all part of the job—and started working on it. But he started making these weird noises, like . . ." Angela raucously and asthmatically breathed in and out, her eyes popping out of her head, ". . . noises like he was having an attack, so I stopped and said, 'What's wrong?' and he said, 'Nothing's wrong, little girl. Just having a good time.' "

"He was so gross," said Rena.

"So," said Angela, "I kept on sucking around his cock and balls, and he kept gasping and howling until it was hard for us both to keep a straight face, even with a mouthful of cock. Rena began to take off his tie and shirt and he said . . . what was it he said to you, Rena?"

"He said, 'You can bite my titties, honey, but not too hard.' "

They laughed. "Oh," said Angela, shaking her head, "he was a real winner. Anyway, we got his clothes off him and steered him to the bedroom. He was moaning and rolling his head around like he was having some sort of seizure. By that time we had his measure—he wanted a little light S and M, obviously—so we would pull on his pubic hair or nip him on the ass. It got to be a kind of game to see how loud we could make him yell. The only thing was, once he got on the bed he started thrashing around so much I was afraid he was going to whack one of us on the side of the head."

"He was a really big guy," added Rena. "It was sort of scary."

"You mean," I asked, "he was thrashing around in pain?"

"Naw," said Angela disdainfully. "Ecstasy. We didn't hurt him really—that's not our scene. There's other girls for that. We just pretended. Pretend is all he wanted. Hell, if we'd hauled off and popped him a couple of time, he'd've called the cops." She laughed, throwing her head back. "His best line was when he got on the bed, and he was moaning and gasping, and he said 'You can handcuff me if you want to.' 'Why would we want to handcuff you?' I asked, which was kind of mean of me. 'Because,' he said, and get this, 'because I want you to make me a prisoner of love.' "

Rena and Angela let off gales of laughter, and I laughed with them, though I felt rather sorry for the poor Texan; he was probably as crude and gross as they said, but it sounded as though he had a rather touching sentimental streak.

"Even without handcuffs," said Angela, "we managed to get his rocks off in pretty short order."

"Uh . . . how did you . . . ?" I asked. My question was more than merely polite.

"How did we make him come?" asked Angela. "I got him on his back and fucked him while Rena sat on his face."

"Oh."

"It was definitely fast-service, junk-food type sex. He was dumb, because he'd paid a lot to be with two girls, and then didn't even know how to use us. Hell, he could've got the same service on Forty-second Street for a lot less money." Her scorn of the Texan was complete.

"Do you usually . . . uh . . . usually work more slowly?"

"Um *hum*," said Angela emphatically. "Most guys that want two chicks are like connoisseurs, you know what I mean? It's like they're wine drinkers as opposed to beer drinkers. They don't just want to get their rocks off, they want a little finesse."

"You mean, they want more than just . . ." I gestured vaguely with my hand.

"Yeah. First of all, they usually like to begin by watching."

"Watching?"

"Yeah. Rena and me start by giving them a little show," she moved closer to Rena and put her arm around her, and nuzzled her neck, all the while keeping her eyes on me and dropping her voice into a seductive range, "something like this . . . we kiss a little . . . and touch each other's tits . . . through our clothes . . . nothing heavy, you understand . . . and maybe stick a tongue in an ear . . . and let our hands kinda fool around down there where the pussy is . . . and all the while we're asking the guy if he's new in New York, and does he like it, and where is he staying, and what does he do for a living. . . ." She continued to play with Rena as she spoke, cupping her breast lightly and massaging the nipple which showed erect through the thin material of her blouse. Rena moved her hand to Angela's crotch and rubbed lightly up and down with a couple of fingers, while her expression grew dreamy.

"And, of course," continued Angela, "we make sure the guy has plenty to drink or smoke or sniff, or whatever it is he's into. Incidentally, do you need a refill?"

"No thanks," I said stiffly. "I'm fine."

"Then, *very* slowly we begin to kind of unbutton and unzip, and start to let a little flesh show. . . ." she opened Rena's blouse and gently pulled it off the shoulder, while Rena undid the top button of Angela's jeans, "then we kind of let the guy get used to flesh in small doses. Of course," Angela said, "if he wants to join us at any time, he's welcome. But usually, the more sensitive ones like to watch for a while." She smiled ingenuously at me.

I wondered for a few minutes whether they were making fun of me. More confusing, I didn't know how I wanted to respond if they were issuing an invitation. A variety of possibilities ran through my head: I could stand up with a jaunty smile and say I had to be going; or I could get huffy and say I was not that kind of girl; or I could look sincere and allow as to how I believed everyone should be allowed to do her own thing. . . . Or I could acknowledge that my pussy was moist and my mouth was dry and I was curious as hell as to what they could do about it. For the time being, I returned Angela's smile with a bland little smile of my own.

Angela leaned over and kissed Rena lightly on the shoulder. "Little by little, we get our clothes off. Sometimes, if the guy's a long time warming up, it can take as much as an hour, or if he's fairly hot to trot we can speed up the process—though we never *rush.*" She slowly unbuttoned Rena's blouse and slipped it off, as Rena simultaneously eased Angela's thin sweater over her head. They sat in their bras facing me. Angela stroked the line of Rena's arm from fingertips to neck with a light touch that I could almost feel myself. "We usually," Angela said innocently, "don't get passionate at this stage of things. We just kind of tease and pose."

Rena giggled and leaned over to kiss Angela's slight cleavage; at the same time she unhooked her bra and guided the straps down her arms. Angela inserted her hand in the top of Rena's jeans and I could see it in outline, molding her crotch. They smiled at each other, then at me, as they continued to touch and caress, like two lovely, languid puppies at play.

I had stopped pretending to smile, and watched with confused fascination. I felt that something was expected of me, but I didn't know what. I still didn't know how I was going to react if ever an out-and-out invitation to join them came. There lurked in my mind the possibility that I wouldn't go through with the scene, though that possibility was growing fainter by the minute.

Angela stood and slipped off her jeans, leaving only her bikini panties, which barely concealed a surprisingly thick tuft of dark brown hair between her legs. Her breasts were small, and the nipples were a deep reddish brown. She knelt on the sofa and Rena grasped each cheek of her small ass with both hands and pulled her crotch to her face. Rena's mouth was open, but she did not touch Angela's pussy, only breathed on it, the way one breathes on a cold window to make it steam. Angela kept her hands on Rena's shoulders as she watched her with bowed head. After a few minutes she pulled back and guided Rena to her feet, then unzipped her jeans and deftly eased them to the floor. Rena was not wearing panties; her ass was as round and rosy as a couple of prize peaches, and when she turned, her deep black pubic hair was sparse and revealed the neat slit between her thighs.

The two girls wrapped their arms around each other and kissed, their tongues darting from mouth to mouth, then they looked at me. "By this time," Angela said, as if she were lecturing, "we usually just kind of drift over to the guy and sort of ease him into the scene." They moved to either side of me. I had worried so much about what I was going to say or do when that moment came; but unnecessarily, for I said and did nothing. Instead, I allowed myself to be absorbed into lovemaking without a second thought.

Angela, sure of herself, slipped her hand into the top of my coveralls and found my breast. Sensitively she explored its circumference with lightly probing fingers, then centered on the nipple with agitating thumb and forefinger. Rena, on the other side, put a hand between my thighs and rubbed up one side, then down the other, in slow motion.

For a few minutes I sat like a lump. Then, tentatively, not looking directly at either, I touched each on the leg. As though it had been the signal she was waiting for, Angela slowly unzipped my coveralls right down to the crotch, and eased my arms free.

"We thought you probably had a dynamite body," she said with an impudent, teasing smile. "All day we kept wondering just what this thing was hiding."

I said nothing as I caressed her cheek, then conscientiously, I touched Rena's cheek with my other hand. Angela unsnapped my bra.

"Ohhh, look at these," she said to Rena. They giggled as each simultaneously bent over and took a nipple in her mouth. The thrill of their touch drew a gasp of surprise from me. Spontaneously I clutched the hair of each head covering my breasts but did not press them closer, for both girls knew exactly the right pressure to create the most pleasure. As their tongues circled and teeth nipped, their hands ran along my sides and belly, and one of them found its way into my crotch.

Along with the pleasure, however, there remained a vestigial uneasiness: I could not forget that I was doing something considered unnatural; most bizarrely, I worried because I was afraid that I was not holding up my end of the bargain, was not properly reciprocating my hostesses' hospitality. A good middle-class Connecticut upbringing can color every aspect of a girl's life.

"What . . . what should I do . . . ?" I whispered.

Both raised their heads and looked questioningly at me. "What do you mean?" asked Angela.

"What do you want me to do?"

They looked blank for an instant, then Angela,

understanding, laughed. "You just leave everything to us. You don't have a thing to worry about." She kissed me on the lips and stood. Rena rose also, and each took one of my hands and pulled me to my feet. The coveralls slipped down around my ankles.

"Step out of those and come with us," said Angela, guiding me toward a door at the far end of the room.

Their bedroom was carpeted in the same blue as the living room, and their bed was kingsized, covered with a white brocaded throw. At the head there was a pile of pillows—square, round, oblong, rectangular—all white, but in various materials and textures. On the wall facing the foot of the bed was a smoked mirror that rose from floor to ceiling.

We stood at the edge of the bed as Angela lowered my panties and then licked between my navel and crotch. Rena stood behind me, cupping my breasts in her hands and nuzzling my neck as she pressed against my back and buttocks. The three of us edged onto the bed, and I lay on my back with my legs hanging over the edge. Rena joined me, her head near mine, her body stretching over the expanse in the opposite direction, while Angela knelt on the floor in the V formed by my open legs.

Angela blew little puffs of breath against my pussy while making whimpering sounds of pleasure. Rena, her lips on mine, tickled both my nipples as I squirmed and twisted. I felt Angela's tongue outlining the crease of my pussy and I spread my legs wider. Rena took her lips from mine and put them between my breasts, then began licking the valley, from one nipple to the other. I moaned and held her head with outstretched fingers. Angela parted the lips between my legs, then her tongue and mouth filled the cavity, drinking in my pussy as she burrowed ever more forcefully into its depths. As she grew more excited, sucking and growling and shaking her face from side to side in her effort to go deeper, Rena took one of my nipples between her teeth and the other in her fingers and squeezed to the point of exquisite pain. I cried out as the sensations merged into an orgasm that ripped through my body like a tornado, and caused my back to arch and toes to curl, and fingers to dig into the white brocade. With a sigh wrenched from my belly, I sank into the bed, exhausted and sated. I lay for a minute with my arm across my eyes, too spent even to worry about satisfying my partners. Then, dutifully, I prepared to do the best I could to bring them the same pleasure they had brought me. I needn't have bothered, for they had formed a sixty-nine and quickly brought each other to orgasm as I watched.

The three of us then lay on the huge bed for a long while. I stared at the ceiling, fatigued, satisfied and a little confused at my lack of guilt, considering the taboo I had violated. Instead of distress I felt immensely warm toward both girls, and the three of us fondled each other as we silently regained our strength.

Angela was the first to speak. "You are one hot number, Diane," she said.

"And you," I replied. Turning to Rena I added, "And you. You're both so terrific. It was just

. . . just great." Then, shyly, I confessed, "I've never done that before."

Both girls laughed. Angela said, "I guess we're just perverts, leading lady photographers astray."

I laughed with them, a little defensively. "I didn't mean to sound so naive."

Angela put her hand over my mouth. "Don't apologize and don't worry. We've had a terrific time together. No words necessary." She got off the bed and asked, "Do you want some more wine?"

"No, thank you. I have to get up early. I ought to go." I sat up and looked at them, so slender and lively, and unconcerned. They pranced around the bedroom in unabashed nakedness, preening and affectionate. I watched them for a few seconds, flooded with gratitude. "Thank you both, so much," I said.

"Don't mention it," said Angela with a playful caress of my nipples. "It was our pleasure."

I went to the living room to step back into my coveralls. I was dressed and at the door in five minutes, no longer. I turned, not sure of the farewell required: did one promise to keep in touch or what? Again Angela took charge. "Listen, I'll give you a call tomorrow about Mark."

"Mark?"

"Yeah. You said you wanted some work behind the camera. Remember? We know someone who might need a photographer."

"Oh, yes. How nice. Thanks."

"I'll ask him if he's got anything going on now, and let you know. OK?"

"That's wonderful," I said. "Thanks again. For

everything." I blew kisses to her and Rena, who was standing behind her, and left.

It had been quite a day. My first assignment and my first lesbian affair. I went home and slept like a log.

Chapter 9

My tea grew cold. I lay on the bed watching the silent TV, the jerky images making no sense without sound to explain them. William's call had begun to rankle; though in the past he had always brought me good news, the tone of his voice on this evening had been ominous and disquieting. I began to take a short inventory of my last four years, letting my eye rove over the photographs—of me and those I had made myself—that I had affixed to my wall like diplomas in a doctor's office. Each indicated a hurdle cleared, acknowledged a triumph or signaled a change of directions. But the gallery was incomplete as a biography. There were, for instance, no pictures of Angela and Rena, and in a curious way those two had had a profound influence on my life. Not that I had an extended affair with them—I never even had sex with them again; they never asked me to—but they did introduce me to Mark Davids, and Mark Davids deflected my course in the surprising way those pop-up shields in pinball machines cause the silver ball to whiz down unexpected channels. There are no pictures of Mark Davids on my wall either; there are probably no pictures of Mark Davids anywhere, because he's a very circumspect man.

The day after I had been with the two girls, Angela called—bright and chipper and as nonchalant as if the evening before had never happened. I still found it hard to disassociate sex from feelings; all my physical encounters left emotional crumbs scattered over my psyche, and I have never been able to greet with casualness someone whose face the night before has been buried in my pussy. Angela (as, I suppose, was Rena) was of a different stripe, and without once making an allusion to our threesome, said, "I called Mark and he said you should call. There might be something for you, if you're interested." She gave me his number, then asked, "Did I tell you very much about him?"

"Not really. Just that he might need a photographer."

"Oh. Well, I guess that sums it up. You can figure out the rest yourself. Listen, I gotta run. Be seeing you. Bye-bye."

"Bye-bye." I hung up, feeling a little slighted.

Later I called the number Angela had given me and a deep, cultivated voice responded. I explained who I was and that I was looking for work, after mentioning Angela.

"Yes," he said thoughtfully. "What have you done so far?"

"Mostly fashion, but also some human interest work and some portraits." I talked fast. "I have a portfolio which I'd like to show you if you have a few minutes. I could drop by right away, or any time."

"You know what sort of things I need?"

"Sure," I lied heartily. "I can come up with anything you're in the market for."

There was a pause on the other end, as I wondered whether I'd overdone it. Finally, he said, "Why don't you drop by with your portfolio, Diane."

"Great," I said. "Where are you located?"

He gave me the address and the time, and I asked, "Is the office under your name?"

His pause seemed significant. "No. It's on the sixteenth floor, under the name of the magazine. Honey Enterprises."

"Oh, of course," I recovered quickly. "See you at three."

I had never heard of a magazine called *Honey*, but they had it at my newsstand. It was a skin publication, pure and simple, that specialized in women's asses. Their centerfold was called the "Honeybuns of the Month," and featured a truly spectacular girl lying on her stomach with her ass—rosy and round and elevated by pillows like a centerpiece on a buffet—the main focus of the photograph. I was nonplused. This was pornography and I was upset at the idea of becoming associated with it; on the other hand, I had absolutely no photographic assignments on my agenda, and I wanted to work more than anything. I decided, oh, what the hell, at least it wouldn't hurt to talk to Mark Davids.

It didn't hurt to talk to Mark Davids. He was a quiet, pipe-smoking, tweedy sort in his thirties, who wore horn-rimmed glasses and chewed his nails. His office might have been found in a rectory or convent, it was so plain and unadorned. As I worked with him, I learned he had created a smokescreen around his career: he liked to tell people at parties he was "in publishing" then push on before they got to specifics. He was living a fantasy as a gentleman publisher.

He was, however, all business at his own magazine. I was ushered into the office by an ordinary-looking fat girl who was trying hard to live up to her good-natured image. Mark rose and extended his hand urbanely, but could not conceal his surprise at seeing me. I made certain he would be surprised: I had got myself up in a red Calvin Klein suit and white silk blouse, and I looked terrific. When in doubt, I fall back on my looks.

He recovered immediately and invited me to sit down. I did so, and put my work portfolio, opened, on his desk. "I'm so pleased to have this chance to meet you," I said brightly.

He nodded, leafing through the book, then looked up. "I don't think you grasp what it is we're after here," he said.

I took a deep breath and plunged in. "Well, I've never done the sort of thing you publish, but that doesn't mean I can't. Look, I've worked with models, and I've worked both in studios and on location. I can certainly give you any kind of photograph you want."

He smiled distantly, unconvinced. "There aren't many women in this business," he said.

"Then it's time there were more." I was like a

dog struggling for a bone I hadn't particularly wanted until I thought someone was going to take it away from me. When I had entered his office I had been more or less indifferent as to whether or not I got a job from him. As Mark remained tepid, I grew determined.

"In this business," he said, "most of the photography is freelance. That is, the photographer does his work and if we—myself and other people in this line of publishing—like it, we buy it. If we don't like it, no go. Now, a few of us sometimes commission special photographers to do work. Not many of the skin magazines do that. I don't do it very often; I don't have to, because there are plenty of guys out there willing to work on spec—to take a chance. If you want to take a chance, that's your business. But frankly, I'd advise against it. You just don't look like you'd be able to hack it in this business." He looked at me ironically and appreciatively and added, "Of course, if you want to pose for us, that's something else." He meant to be conventionally gallant, but I seized on his remark.

"That's insulting," I said coldly. I really wasn't angry—I never am when people compliment my looks, no matter how indirectly—but I thought I could climb upon a high horse and shame Mark Davids into reconsidering. "You assume just because I'm a woman I'm not capable of taking a picture of an ass or two. That's a very chauvinistic attitude, Mr. Davids."

Most men in his position would have shown me the door and not given the matter another thought. Poor Mark, as I was to learn, had a conscience, and was torn between his profession and his image of himself; an enlightened publisher, even of skin mags, couldn't be a male chauvinist pig. He studied me forlornly before saying, "Well, I suppose you could try." He wasn't really offering me any more than a chance to take a risk with my own time and money. But I didn't understand that right away.

Instantly I changed back into a demure, eye-batting beauty and gushed, "Oh, thank you. You really won't regret it."

As it turned out, neither of us regretted it. I borrowed a studio that week and did a series of shots of a black girl—a dancer from a topless bar off Forty-second Street—that were as sizzling as anything *Honey*'s fans had ever seen. Even I was surprised at how well I had done, and was tempted to take credit in the magazine under my own name. Mark thought it might not look right to have a woman photographer photographing a woman erotically—he was more concerned about upsetting his readers than protecting my reputation—so I called myself D. Bourne.

As D. Bourne, I became a fairly regular contributor to the magazine and gradually branched out until I was selling a small trickle of work to other skin publications.

So, after three years in New York, I was juggling three careers: as model, fashion photographer, and skin photographer. Most of my income came from modeling and that was what took the greater part of my efforts; but the more successful I became, the more I felt that posing in front of the camera was encroaching on my time behind it and I began to resent my assignments. I was not so foolish, however, as to sabatoge the reputation I had built as a model; I was earning top money and needed every cent of it, because I had take an apartment on Central Park West that doubled as a studio and, when my work for the skin magazines picked up, I took a smaller, much cheaper space downtown where I could work without being subject to curious doormen or assistants. Most skin photographers work one on one, so the austere downtown layout was no drawback.

The money I was getting from photography allowed me to do a little better than break even; the money from modeling made sure I didn't have to scrounge. Also, my work as a model nourished my self-esteem; every time I appeared in print or before a camera, it seemed as though that ugly awkward child who dwelled within me was further diminished. At the same time I was able to withstand the inevitable rejections—still all too common, even for an established top model—because I could console myself with the certainty of someday becoming a full-time photographer who didn't have to rely on other people's approval of my looks to earn a living. But time was my enemy; I never seemed to have enough of it. Not only the hours doing the actual modeling, but the go-sees, the frantic rushing from one booking to the next, all consumed great chunks of my life. One of my dreams was that there was surely some way to simplify all the chores that were necessary before posing, though I never really believed it likely.

Then William made just such a dream come true.

I had kept in touch with William during my three years in the city, or rather, he had kept in touch with me. He called from California every six weeks or so, to chat and ask how I was doing. He took an almost proprietorial interest in my career, and once teasingly said he felt responsible for me, since he had been instrumental in luring me to the big city with its wicked ways. It was a pseudo-joke, a truth thinly disguised with nervous laughter. He had such a strong sense of responsibility that he did worry when I seemed down and caught my gaiety when things were going well. Not that I told him very much about my life; hardly any more than I told my parents. Certainly I never mentioned the skin mags, and he had only the vaguest idea of my fashion photography; I believe he thought it was some sort of hobby for me.

Our exchanges were almost impersonal, rather like formal notes that would have been written between acquaintances a century earlier. We talked about the pleasant things in our lives: I told him a lot about the Griffin campaign and the other plums I had earned and he told me about Helen's winning an amateur tennis championship and their new baby boy (I sent a silver cup from Griffin's inscribed with the child's name, which was also William). I think that for William I was a glamorous figure—a top model whose picture, if not name, was nationally known. For me, William was a decent, sweet presence, rather like a distant, older brother.

During those three years we saw each other only

twice. Once, on their way to Europe, Helen and William had a stopover at Kennedy Airport, and I rushed out with a bottle of champagne; the other time William, again with Helen, had flown to New York to meet one of his clients and they were staying only three days. I had drinks with them at the Sherry Netherland. Both times Helen was poised and correct, though hardly warm. William was solicitous and charming and concerned, and seemed intent on not holding my eye for more than a second or two at a time. I came away from both meetings with the idea lodged in the back of my mind that there was a potential between us that would never be developed—rather like a pool of oil too deep ever to be drilled for. I felt pleasantly melancholy after these meetings and, to a lesser extent, after the conversations.

There was no pleasant melancholy, however, after the call William made one night in early September of last year.

After saying hello and asking how I was in a perfunctory and excited voice, he plunged right into the purpose of the call. "One of our clients is the advertising firm of Wade and Thomas, and one of *their* clients is Bin-Bin Beads. You ever hear of them?"

"No. Not of the agency or the beads."

"Well, the agency is a good one and Bin-Bin is just getting established here. They're costume jewelers."

"You mean they make junk jewelry—like in Woolsworth's?"

William gave a little gasp and said, half-jokingly, "For God's sake don't ever use that term again. It's *costume* jewelry or *fashion* jewelry. Don't you forget it."

"OK." I laughed at his seriousness. "Whatever you say. But who's going to care what I call it?"

"The Bin-Bin people will care. A lot. Bin-Bin Beads is a French outfit that's launching their line over here. The head of the U.S. branch lives in California and they went to Wade and Thomas for a campaign, and W&T wants to hire an exclusive model to be the Bin-Bin Bead Girl. . . . Is this beginning to make sense to you?"

"I'm beginning to get your drift, yes," I said lightly. I found it hard to take anything to do with junk jewelry very seriously. In my mind's eye, all I could see were those strands of garish plastic beads on aluminum racks in the five-and-ten stores.

"The Bin-Bin people are very picky, and they've turned down candidate after candidate. I urged the W&T team to show them your Griffin ads, and when the big honcho, whose name is Pierre Duplessis, saw your pictures he said, 'Voilà!' "

"Oh, William," I laughed. "Surely real Frenchmen don't say 'Voilà.' "

"This one did. He not only said 'Voilà,' he bunched his fingers and kissed the tips, just like in the movies."

"Sounds like an impostor."

"He's the real thing. Real enough to sink several million dollars into a nationwide campaign to launch their line."

"Is he going to want to look me over?" I asked, still not very impressed.

"Maybe, eventually. But first he wants the head of the team at W&T to check you out. A guy named Harry Ort is the exec in charge. He lives in New York and will be in touch with you tomorrow or the next day. That's Harry Ort the Third."

"Harry Ort the Third?" I giggled. "You'd think they'd give up after the first one, wouldn't you? What a name."

"It's an old New England family, Diane," said William almost reprovingly. Then, his voice becoming more serious he added, "You know, I'd really like to do something for you, something you'd like. I hope this works out. It could be a big jump for you."

I was touched. "Thanks, William. You've already been such a big help. I appreciate it."

There was an awkward silence, then we rather self-consciously started chatting about Helen and their son, who was a little over a year old. Finally we hung up, and I didn't give Bin-Bin Beads another thought.

The next day I got a call from Harry Ort III, who politely invited me to drop by the offices of Wade and Thomas.

I went that afternoon. Harry Ort III had a corner office facing Madison Avenue that was done up like an English manor drawing room: oak paneling, brass chandelier, maroon leather sofa and hunting prints. Harry Ort III fit right in with his conservative navy blue suit, striped tie and white shirt. He was tall and somewhere between thirty-five and forty-five; exercise and massage had given him a healthy pink glow under his waning summer tan, and his hair was uniformly dark brown, though that might have been touched up. His eyes were brown and assessing, and his smile—on full sensual lips—was slightly mocking, as though he didn't want to be thought too friendly. He stood as I entered and held out his hand.

"Miss Bourne," he said with his deep voice and Ivy League accent. "It's a pleasure to meet you."

I shook his hand demurely and replied, "Thank you. What a nice office."

"Yes," he said, glancing casually around as though he were just noticing it. "I brought a few things from home to make it a little more personal. I spend so much of my time here. . . ." He shrugged, looking me over closely. It was hard for me to tell whether he liked what he saw.

"It's awfully important to enjoy your surroundings," I said. The conversation was stilted, but neither of us was paying any attention to it. Instead, we were sizing each other up, each of us wondering how to handle the other.

"I understand you're a friend of William Allen. Salt of the earth, William," said Harry Ort III.

"Oh, yes, we've known each other for years." Then I added, in order to dispel any wrong ideas, "And Helen and the baby are two of my favorite people."

"I've never met Mrs. Allen or their child." Harry looked at me thoughtfully. I suspect he would have found it impossible to repeat what either of us had just said, he was so obviously distracted. He cleared his throat and changed his tone. "Well, you've heard about Bin-Bin Beads? And the Bin-Bin Bead Girl?"

"The beads yes, the girl no."

"We're looking for a model to become the Bin-Bin Bead Girl. An exclusive contract. It could be a very big job for the right girl."

"Bin-Bin is a curious name."

"Family name. The founder was Jean-Luc Bin-Bin over a hundred years ago. Bin-Bin Bijoutiers are quite well known in France."

"And now they want to become well known here."

"Right. They're quality. Great stuff. Are you familiar with their jewelry?"

"No. I've never seen a Bin-Bin Bead, at least not to recognize it." At first I found it hard to discuss Bin-Bin Beads with a straight face.

Harry Ort got up and went to a side table on which a case was sitting. He brought it back to his desk. "Here are some of their things," he said, watching me as he opened it.

The colors were glowing jewellike reds and greens and ambers, and there were massive and delicate settings: earrings, bracelets, brooches, necklaces—all sparkled in the light of the desk lamp. I picked up a necklace of simulated rubies interspersed with beaten gold leaves and held it before me.

"Very pretty," I said.

"Yes. The best of its kind. We need a woman who can wear jewelry like that with style. Not everyone can."

"No, I guess not," I said noncommittally.

"At first we wanted someone young, like that kid who does the jeans ads, but we decided anyone that age wouldn't have the sophistication to carry it off."

"Hmm."

"Also, we have to be careful to get the right kind of woman. No really high-fashion type because, after all, we're appealing to a mass market. We need someone most women can identify with. But, of course, she has to be the sort of woman most women would want to look like."

"I see."

"And we have to get someone who's wholesome looking enough to appeal as much to Middle America as to the big cities. There's no limiting our market."

"Very interesting."

"Is it?"

"I beg your pardon?"

"Is it very interesting? Are you interested?"

I remained cool. "Of course, I'm interested in learning exactly what you need."

"It would be an exclusive contract. We'd work the terms out with your agency, but I can assure you we'd pay the highest price for your exclusive services."

I hid my excitement. An exclusive contract would mean I was the property of Bin-Bin Beads, but at the same time it would mean no more go-sees or frantic rushing from booking to booking. I would be getting a lot of money for less work. This would give me time I needed to work more on photography. I wanted the job, but I was experienced enough not to show it. I smiled with calculated openness and said, "I appreciate being considered."

"In all honesty," he said, with the dishonest look that frequently accompanies such reassurance, "I have to tell you there are several other candidates."

I was disappointed, but I didn't show that either. "That's understandable," I said blithely.

"However, I'm in a position to recommend strongly the final choice."

"That must be difficult for you."

"You could make it a lot easier."

"How so?"

"By having dinner with me this evening."

We looked at each other across the desk. Neither of us revealed much. I'm not sure what Henry Ort III was thinking at that moment, but I was wondering whcther I should risk throwing him a fuck in order to get the job, or whether that would be the wrong move.

"That's very kind of you," I said. "Actually, I have a date . . . but I guess I could break it." I had made my decision.

"Great," he said, standing. "Shall I pick you up at eight?"

"Fine." I smiled good-bye.

As soon as I hit the sidewalk, I had doubts. One of the great myths of modeling is that you can screw your way into a job. Actually, it's more likely that you can screw your way out of one. If an agency or a client thinks you're right for their product, you can show up with a zipper on your pussy and no one will dare hold it against you. On the other hand, if client or agency or both don't like you, you can go down on every member of the organization and still end up out of luck. There's too much money at stake to play private sexual games.

But there are those borderline cases in which you can't help thinking that just maybe it wouldn't hurt, maybe it really is a close decision, and if I play along I stand a better chance to get the job. It's a feeling that's bred from the chronic insecurity of models, who never—no matter how established, and no matter how beautiful—never feel they're established and beautiful enough, because we all know that rejection is more likely than not. It was during just such a failing of nerve that I had accepted the invitation of Harry Ort III; that he wasn't bad looking also influenced my decision.

By the time he picked me up, I had resigned myself to carrying out my part of the bargain. If Harry Ort wanted to fuck, then fuck we would; that was the agreement implicit in my acceptance. I noted, wryly, that the only thing he was promising was to swing a little influence—hardly, from my point of view, a fair exchange.

In spite of my reservations, the date got off to a pleasant start. Harry was smooth: his manners were impeccable, his conversation light and amusing, and his taste rich. During dinner at Lutece, he never overtly mentioned sex, though in retrospect I can understand that some of his allusions were aimed in that direction.

Once, when the waiter was a few seconds late in refilling our wine glasses and had rushed up to rectify his oversight, Harry laughingly said to me,

"If he lets that happen again, you can punish him." I smiled; the remark seemed good-natured, and I was only mildly confused about his meaning. Later, as we were getting into a taxi, I accidentally stepped on his foot and he said, "Ouch. You're going to pay for that." He took my hand and tapped it lightly with his own. Neither incident had much significance at the time.

We finished dinner about eleven and since it was too early to go to a disco, Harry suggested we "kill a little time" at his place, which was nearby. I went along with the charade. His apartment was on Third Avenue, about a five-minute ride from the restaurant. It was one of those boxy, graceless buildings with useless balconies on which no one ever stands, where apartments begin at two thousand a month.

The living room of Harry's apartment was like his office; he—or more probably, some decorator—had imposed English country on Manhattan stone and steel and picture window. But it was not unpleasant, with its deep leather couches, thick carpeting and heavy drapes.

"What can I get you to drink?" he asked as he put on a record by the Doors.

"Oh, I think just a Perrier, if you have it," I said.

He didn't urge anything stronger on me, nor did he seem annoyed when I refused a toke from the joint he brought in lit from another room. He settled on the couch near me and tapped his foot to the music for a few moments as he sucked in and held the smoke. We talked for a while—about apartments in New York, a subject that has replaced the weather as a general icebreaker—and Harry said, "Well, I was certainly lucky to find this one. The walls are thicker than most."

"You are lucky," I agreed. "There's nothing more annoying than someone else's noise."

He laughed. "I don't mind hearing other people. I'd be worried, though, if I thought they could hear me. I've even soundproofed my game room."

"That was very thoughtful of you," I said.

He laughed again, looking significantly at me, as though I should understand there was a subtler meaning to his remarks. "It's discreet, not thoughtful," he said.

I didn't understand what he was getting at, so I smiled.

"Would you like to see my game room?" he asked.

"Sure," I replied with the lively interest one simulates when an offer to see someone's apartment is made. I got to my feet.

Harry took my hand and gave me another long look, then led me through a door behind the couch. For a moment—as I faced a large fourposter bed with crimson draperies—I thought he had coyly been referring to his bedroom as the game room. But he led me past the bed to a wall of books and pressed against it. Part of the bookcase glided silently open to reveal a dark hole beyond. Harry led me through. I could not make out much of anything and was hesitant to follow him. Then he switched on a dim red light and simultaneously closed the wall.

It was black. Floor, walls and ceiling were all black, and I couldn't see the door we had just come through. As my eyes adjusted to the feeble red glow I saw a low platform in the middle of the room—which was quite small, not much larger than a standard New York bathroom—and things hanging along the walls.

I was frightened, and wanted to leave. Harry stood behind me and gently grasped both my arms. His lips almost touching my ear, he whispered, "This is where I play."

I didn't respond, but stood stiffly in front of him, my mind racing. Should I demand he open the door? At the same time I was curious, even though my stomach felt hollow and I was holding my breath. I was, for a few seconds, immobilized. Harry apparently had met with that reaction before, because he began reassuring me with his cultivated voice. "This is my little hideaway. I've got a few toys . . . nothing very elaborate . . . would you like to try a couple?" The question was posed with such a matter-of-fact politeness that I was thrown off balance.

"I don't know," I answered truthfully.

"Here," he said, taking something off a peg on the wall. He held a strip of silver-studded black leather. "Let's see how you look in this." Before I could say anything he had circled my throat with it and fastened it, like a dog collar. The feel of the leather against my skin was cool and not unpleasant. My stomach was still hollow, and I could hear my heartbeat. He unzipped my dress and eased it over my head, folded it neatly and put it in the corner. Then he unsnapped my bra and put it on top. He took off his jacket, tie and shirt and arranged it all in an equally neat pile beside my clothes. His skin was smooth and hairless in the reddish light.

Neither of us spoke. I stood like a mannequin, not sure of whether I liked what was happening or not. One thing was certain: Harry was in control of the situation.

He took another, more elaborate piece of black leather off a peg and held it before me, then rubbed it against my breasts and stomach. "Hold out your arms," he said softly.

I did so, and he slipped a harness over them that criss-crossed between my breasts and fastened in back with a buckle. "Is that too tight?" he asked solicitously.

"No." I was scarcely able to get the word out. How was I to know what was too tight?

He tugged on the harness a couple of times, hard enough to make me sway. He took off my pantyhose and had me step out of them and my high heels together. "Put the shoes back on," he directed after he had put the pantyhose on top of my other clothes.

He removed his own pants, underwear, shoes and socks, then put on a pair of high black boots which gleamed dully, picking up red highlights from the single bulb above the platform. His cock was semi-hard and his balls hung heavily behind it.

"Sit here," he said in a less gentle voice, pointing to the platform.

I did as I was told; my head came even with his crotch as he stood in front of me. "Do you like those balls?" he asked aggressively.

"Yes."

"What do you want to do with those balls?"

I didn't know what to answer.

"What do you want to do with those balls?" he repeated, then added, "Don't you want to tie those balls up?"

With that coaching, I replied, "Yes."

He took a long leather thong from the wall and handed it to me. "Then I'll let you tie my balls," he said gruffly.

Gingerly at first I began to wrap the thong around his scrotum. He took my hands and guided them, making them pull the thong tighter than I would have on my own. "That's right," he said. "At least you're good for something. What else are you good for?"

There comes a point in all sexual scenes, I suppose, where one can stop or permit them to go on, which means simply that one can cooperate or not. (Of course, I'm not talking about dealings with psychopaths, of which, thank God, I've had none.) Harry's question brought us to that point. I could have laughed and said, "Oh, come off it," and the mood would have been shattered. But by the time he asked, "What else are you good for?" I had been drawn into his fantasy, and I was his willing—though still frightened—accomplice.

"I don't know," I answered weakly in a little-girl voice that surprised me.

"I'll tell you what you're good for, bitch." He

grasped my head by the hair and shoved my face near his cock, which was large, circumcised and smelled incongruously of expensive scented soap. "You're good for sucking my cock." He shoved the head into my mouth and demanded, "Like it?"

"Ummm," was all I could say with my mouth full. I grasped his buttocks—smooth and hard as the rest of him—with both hands to steady myself as I sat on the platform, while he slowly pumped back and forth into my mouth.

After a few minutes he took a fistful of my hair and held my head back, away from his cock; I had so completely entered the game that I felt he was denying me gratification. "That's all you're going to get for now," he said. "If you're good, you can lick it later. Are you going to be good?"

"Yes."

From the wall he took a black leather hood and fitted it over his head. It covered the upper half of his face, with only two slits for eyes, and outlined his skull. In his hand he held a leather riding crop—thin and supple—which he switched a couple of times through the air, making a sharp hissing noise that caused my flesh to congeal. He took another object off the wall and harshly commanded, "Stand up."

He fixed a silver studded leather garter belt around my waist, with clips dangling uselessly against my front and back thighs; then he circled my wrists and ankles with padded leather cuffs, each clipped quickly into place as I stood silently facing him. The leather felt like cold flesh, and caused me to shiver with a mingling of fear and anticipation. I didn't know what to expect, and in a curious way this uncertainty was part of my excitement. For I was excited by now, not merely frightened.

He took hold of the collar around my throat and led me to the center of the platform. "Get on your knees," he said, keeping his hand on the collar, guiding my head down until it was again level with his crotch. His cock was hard and sprang straight from his scented pubic hair. His balls, squeezed against his scrotum by the pressure of the thong, bulged round and hairy between his smooth, almost hairless thighs. He lightly ran the tip of the riding crop up and down my spine, making me shiver, not so much from the cool touch of the leather as from the fear he would suddenly thwack it against my bare hide. I was a part of his fantasy, and had willed myself to be subservient to his caprices; but in doing so I had not lost my instinct for self-protection, nor even my sense of dignity. It was the tension between these two elements, his power over me and my ego—that caused my sensations. I suppose I was experiencing pleasure, for want of a better word.

With his whip he tapped my head lightly, and said, "Get on all fours." I did so. "Now get down and kiss my boots." I lowered my head even further until my lips came in contact with the shiny leather and kiss my boots." I lowered my head even farther he said. "Lick 'em." I was kneeling now, and supporting myself on my elbows as I lowered my head to the floor, and raised my ass. I felt the riding crop trace the cleft between the cheeks of my ass as it passed slowly and lightly back and forth across my anus, causing the sphincter to contract in dread and expectation. As my tongue flicked across the shiny leather of his toes, the riding crop strayed from the crack of the fleshly buns and lightly tapped first one then the other. Suddenly, the whip came down sharply, stingingly, against my flesh. I gasped, but before I could say anything, he recommenced the soothing exploration with the tip of the crop; it now felt like the lightest of massages.

We had passed another barrier. I could have stopped the scene, said, "I'm not into this," and we would probably have had orgasms and called it a night. I sensed this, but I was unwilling to take responsibility for my behavior, or his. One of the curious sources of my pleasure was my willful loss of control—which was the strongest fantasy of the evening. When I accepted the sting of the whip, I had passively moved into a more advanced sphere of our relationship.

"Lick 'em like you enjoy it, bitch," he said, keeping the crop roving over my buttocks. Again there was a sudden sting as the crop swished through the air and connected with my flesh; the sudden sting made me whimper. "What's the matter, cunt? Didn't you like that?"

"No," I had to answer, although neither yes nor no was entirely truthful.

"Then do what I tell you to. Be a good girl, or it'll happen again."

"What do you want me to do?"

"What do you want to do?"

"Anything you say." This was not true, but I did not want to relinquish my passivity to the point of naming my own torment. I wanted him to control that. Furthermore, I was so inexperienced in this type of sex I didn't know what to ask for.

"Anything I say? Then I'm your master?"

"Yes."

The whip continued to roam around my ass, down the crevice, over the cheeks, with sinister pauses that made me shiver as I projected the sting that might follow.

"Put your hands behind your back."

To do so I had to lay my cheek against the leather-sheathed mat that covered the floor of the platform. He stepped beside me and connected the two cuffs he had put on my wrists. I heard the rattle of a chain as he took some device from the wall. The sound heightened my fear and expectation, as he pushed my legs farther apart and clamped what seemed to be a metal bar to the cuffs on my ankles to keep them separated. He dragged a chilling heavy chain between the cheeks of my ass and clamped it to my wrists, then snapped each end to one of my ankles. This chain was purely for aesthetic effect, for it was not employed further.

He stood behind me and kneaded my ass, cupping the cheeks roughly in his palms. Suddenly he smacked my ass with his open palm; the loud explosion of flesh against flesh was more startling than the pain, which was not very great, but significant enough to make me jerk.

"What's the matter, bitch? Didn't you deserve that?"

"Yes."

"Then why did you whine?"

"I don't know."

"You don't know." He mimicked my little girl voice. "I don't like noisy cunts. I'm gonna make sure you don't yell again."

I hadn't yelled, but if that was part of his fantasy, it was now also part of mine.

He lifted my head and stuck a round white ball attached to a black leather band into my mouth, and buckled the catch behind my ears. My teeth clamped the ball as my mouth was forced into an O around it. The only sound I could make was the "Ahhh" of deaf-mutes.

He returned behind me, where my ass was sticking in the air, an object for his pleasure. He grasped both cheeks and squeezed, then ran a finger back and forth over the anus. With his thumbs he separated the cheeks and stuck his finger a little way into the hole. I moaned.

"That hurt?" he asked mockingly. "You think that little finger hurts, what you going to think when I stick my cock up there?" He poked a little harder, making me groan and wiggle. I heard him unscrew a jar, and next felt smooth grease being rubbed around my anus, then his finger slipped into the hole much more readily, and almost pleasurably. At the same time he reached beneath me with his other hand and inserted a finger into my pussy.

He positioned himself on his knees behind me. I felt, again with dread and anticipation, his legs against mine, then his thick hot cock, rubbing up and down in the crevice he had titillated with his riding crop. He raised himself over me and brought the head of his cock to my asshole, and slowly, slowly began to insert it.

The pain was strong enough to make me groan. If I could have talked I might have told him to stop. But I couldn't do more than make sounds, and these seemed to excite him further. Relentlessly, though slowly, millimeter by millimeter, he pushed his cock further into my hole. He would pause every few seconds and agitate my pussy with his finger, as though bestowing a reward for each inch of flesh his cock devoured. Deeper and deeper he moved, inexorably delving into my guts.

"This is tight, baby. This is good. You got some ass, baby. This ass mine?" He kept up a breathless litany, extolling my asshole, as he eased his way into it, right up to the root of his cock. I felt as though he were going to tear the flesh, and yet I still don't know whether I would have stopped him if I could have. Along with the pain there was an incredible excitement and a surge of warmth through my pussy.

"It's all the way in, baby. You got my cock, baby. I'm gonna fuck your ass. I'm gonna fuck your tight ass." He began to move up and down, slowly pulling his cock up until the head was almost out, then with a groan he would enter again, pressing all the way in until I felt his balls rubbing against my thigh. In and out he moved, faster and faster, until he was pumping up and down in rhythm that matched my accelerated heartbeat.

He came quickly and noisily, with a great howl of teeth-gritting pleasure. His finger found my clit and brought me to a shivering, explosive orgasm. We rested, united, panting heavily.

Slowly—and painfully for me—he took his

cock out of my ass, then unhooked my hands and feet and fell, exhausted, to the platform. He made me stretch out alongside him, my back to him, and put his arms around me with tenderness, cupping my breasts in each hand. He snuggled closer and in a few seconds fell asleep. I dozed off too.

I don't know how long we slept, but it probably was no more than fifteen or twenty minutes. When I awoke, I was conscious that he was kissing the back of my neck, and that our bodies had become welded together by their mingled sweat.

"Are you all right?" he asked, when he saw I was awake. He unfastened the dog collar around my neck.

"Fine," I said. My ass was sore, but that surely was to be expected. "And you?"

"I'm just great," he whispered into my ear. He kissed my neck and turned me so that our lips could meet. He had removed his hood, and his hair was boyishly tousled. He caressed my breasts. "You're so beautiful," hc said.

I smiled my thanks. With a sigh he began to remove the rest of the paraphernalia he had decked me with: the garter belt, cuffs and chain. Then he untied the thong around his balls and took off his boots. He was transformed back into a preppie-type who lived among English hunting prints. In a very few minutes we both looked a little out of place in the all-black, red-tinted game room. Harry gathered our clothes and said, "Why don't we get dressed in the bedroom?" making the suggestion sound like a formal invitation.

I followed him through the opening in the wall

which appeared when he touched it, and watched from the other side as the false bookcase slid back into place, giving no clue of the room beyond.

He placed our clothes on the fourposter and turned to embrace me, kissing me with quick little pecks on my lips and cheeks and eyes, as though he were tentatively edging into foreplay. I was confused, wondering whether he was working up to a more conventional fuck than the one he had performed. I was not particularly taken with that possibility.

"Do you know what I'd like to do sometime?" he asked.

"No, what?"

"I'd like to spend the night with you and just cuddle." He kissed me again. "You're so beautiful. I'd like to cuddle all night long." His voice as well as his smile took on an adolescent innocence.

"That would be nice," I said without much enthusiasm. I was ready to go home and be alone.

"I wish we could do it tonight, but I've got an early meeting. It wouldn't be fair to you," he said, nibbling my ear.

"Some other time," I whispered gratefully, feeling relieved.

"Umm. Some other time."

I began to dress and so did he. "You don't have to take me home," I said. "I'll just grab a cab."

He looked surprised and even outraged. "I'm not about to let you out alone in this city," he said. "Of course I'll see you home." He sounded stuffy, and as he put back on his dark suit and wing-tip shoes he resumed the persona of Ivy League advertising executive which he had shed beyond the bookcase wall. By the time he had knotted his striped tie he was again Harry Ort III, and he escorted me to my apartment door and said good night with a peck on the cheek. He did add, with uncharacteristic fervor, "It was wonderful, Diane. Thank you."

"For me, too," I said, my hand on his cheek.

In a more honest moment I would not have called the evening wonderful, but it had not been dull. I wondered whether I ever wanted to see Harry Ort III's game room again. As I shut my apartment door I thought, not for a while, at least.

Chapter 10

William called two days later, excitement bubbling through his voice like sparkling water. "I want to be the first to tell you," he said. "You got the job!"

In spite of my efforts to control my expectations, I had nervously been waiting for some word. I never thought, though, that it would come so quickly and so positively. The most I could hope for, I thought, would be that the head of the American branch of Bin-Bin Beads would want to see me. I never dreamed that I would be chosen without a lot more interviews.

"Are you sure?" I asked. "I mean, I've only seen one guy. . . ."

"Yeah, and you didn't even have to see him, as it turns out, because he's been taken off the account and another exec who lives out here on the West Coast has been assigned to it. So he can work more closely with Mr. Duplessis."

"You mean," I asked, "that Harry Ort III is out of the picture?"

"He was never very much in the picture. Wade and Thomas made the decision to switch the whole Bin-Bin operation out here several days ago.

"But I was interviewed by Mr. Ort."

"Lag. Time lag. Sorry to have wasted your time."

"You mean his recommendation isn't what got me the job?"

"Nope. I don't believe he's been asked for a recommendation. Just your own beautiful self got the job. Mr. Duplessis and the new exec, Ben Toliver, went over your print work and ran your TV commercials and decided that you were the Bin-Bin Bead Girl."

"Don't they want to meet me?"

"Of course they want to meet you, but only as a formality. As Ben explained it to me, Mr. Duplessis feels that it doesn't matter so much what you look like in person; what's important is how you come across in the media, and he thinks you come across as the Bin-Bin Bead Girl. He sees you as beautiful and wholesome, and I was able to vouch for your character and tell him you were just as upstanding as you were beautiful."

We both laughed. "Does that really matter?" I asked. He grew serious. "Actually, it does. Mr. Duplessis said he wanted to make sure the Bin-Bin Bead Girl wasn't prone to scandal. He's right, of course, because he's peddling his jewelry in every corner of the country—the Bible Belt and Middle America and all those other hard-nosed places—as well as the cities. But there's no sweat. As the lawyer for W&T, I was able to swear absolutely that you didn't do drugs and were morally impeccable. I was right, wasn't I?"

"Of course," I said laughing. It was the truth.

"I'm to happy for you, Diane," said William, ". . . and, uh, so's Helen. We're both so pleased about this."

"I hardly know how to thank you. For everything. You've been just . . . just. . . ." Tears welled in my eyes, and they could be heard in my voice.

"Now, listen, don't get carried away," he said, attempting lightness, but he was moved also. "You did this all on your own. I just kind of smoothed the way. You're such a terrific girl, something like this had to happen."

I was crying. "Oh, William, all I can say is thanks, and that's not nearly enough."

"It's more than I deserve. It really is. We'll talk later, OK?" He hung up before he broke down too.

I bawled like a baby for a few minutes, then giggled, then called Harold Ames at the agency to tell him the news.

From then on everything happened fast. I was flown to the coast for two days to meet Mr. Duplessis and Ben Toliver. We were together for a total of maybe two hours at most. I met some of the other executives from Bin-Bin Beads, most of them laid-back California types who seemed to appeal to the very French Mr. Duplessis. I didn't even have the chance to see William, because he was tied up in some negotiations that made it necessary for him to be in San Francisco. I did call Helen, who congratulated me warmly, but made no effort to meet me, and then I flew back.

Within two weeks, I was filming commercials. The first was shot on location, and I was dressed in sporty sweater and skirt and had to run along a fenced-in meadow while, on the other side of the fence, a horse trotted at my side. I was wearing beads and a bracelet and earrings—simple fake pearls—and I had to race into the camera, stop as the jewelry was highlighted and say, "Bin-Bin Beads make you *happy*!" It took two days for my part of the thirty-second commercial, and I don't know how much more time to put the rest of the film together—the part in which the narrator extolls the old-world craftsmanship, the real jewel glow, etc., etc. At the end, though, everyone was wildly enthusiastic.

The next one was shot in a studio, where I was placed in a gondola, wearing a mask and a hooded black evening cape and dangling fake diamonds in my ears, at my throat and on my wrists, and had to confide with a low, sidelong glance, "Bin-Bin Beads make you *mysterious*." In one commercial, I was surrounded by men at what was supposed to be every middle-class cocktail party in Middle America. I was wearing a reasonably modest blue party dress and simple earrings with blue stones and matching clips, and as the camera panned in I looked up, surprised, and said, "Bin-Bin Beads make you *popular*!" Then there was the one in the red dress: "Bin-Bin Beads make you *beautiful*!"

In conjunction with the television spots there were print ads of a corresponding theme that ran in most national magazines. As soon as the ads began to appear, I was recognized and people stopped on the street to stare or craned in restaurants. At the same time, I was earning a great deal of money and was modeling less. Just as I'd hoped, I had more time to work on my photography.

There was a drawback, however. The more famous I became as the Bin-Bin Bead Girl, the more resistance I met as a fashion photographer. This was partly because of jealousy, I think, but also because many art directors just couldn't take me seriously while I was appearing on every channel and in every publication in the country. When I did get assignments, I frequently met hostility from other models who didn't like the idea that I was working both sides of the camera. There was a lot of distrust and uneasiness swirling around me.

So, though I had more time, I didn't have correspondingly more fashion work to fill it with. I turned to the skin mags.

The art directors and publishers of these magazines were rather pleased to have a known model freelancing for them, even if I was incognito. And the models—some of whom were recommended by the magazine—were doing the work only for the money, and didn't invest much of their egos in the projects. They were mostly broke and eager to get through the assignments with as little hassle as possible, so there were no snotty remarks or attempted put-downs. The pay for the skin mags was miserable, but at this stage I wasn't in the game for the money but the experience; Bin-Bin Beads was subsidizing my photographic education.

In spite of my prominence—my being recognized, written about and interviewed ("Bin-Bin Bead Girl Widely Read" was the title of one absolutely insane article in an afternoon tabloid)—I still didn't have much of a social life. I simply couldn't afford the time that other models put into late nights at Xenon or the Mudd Club or Elaine's. Occasionally I felt lonely, and I also could, when down, work myself into a state of semi-guilt about my promiscuity, but for the most part I was pleased with my life. The main reason for my satisfaction was that it remained a life in flux—something I was creating. I was not just a model who would be burned out in a few years, but a budding photographer. Futhermore, I was a photographer who was versatile enough to do both fashion and porn, soft and hard. I remained deliciously uncommitted to any one definite course of action. I was hovering near a lack of responsibility, if not actually reveling in it. Aided by circumstances, I was avoiding commitment.

The fortunes of Harold Ames as the owner of my agency, and Anita, as my booker, had risen with mine. I wouldn't say we were exactly close, but certainly there was a good feeling among us. Obviously they were familiar with every facet of my modeling career, and knew something about the fashion photography, but nothing at all about the skin mags. Both Harold and Anita pampered me after I became the Bin-Bin Bead Girl; partially, because I was a valuable property, but also, because they were nice people who really liked me.

"I'm worried about you, Diane," Harold said one afternoon in his office. Anita, sitting facing me, solemnly nodded her agreement, showing that both had been discussing the matter before my arrival.

"Why?" I asked. I had just made an appearance at a department store as the Bin-Bin Bead Girl and was flushed with the approval of the crowd that had turned out to meet me.

"I think—Anita and I both think—you're not relaxing enough."

"Do I look tense?" I asked worriedly, and my hands automatically went to the corners of my eyes, where I thought I had seen the beginnings of wrinkles.

"No, no. You look great. Never better," Harold said. "You seem as healthy as . . . as a cow—no comparison intended, you understand." He smiled slightly, his gaze still, after almost four years, directed to the side of my head and not into my eyes. "It's just that we've noticed, couldn't help but notice, that you don't see many people for fun. Now," he raised his hand as I started to speak, "I know that your personal life is none of our business, and that you have . . . ah . . . some outside interests, what with your photography, and so on, but you should really take advantage of your position."

"What is my position?"

"You're one of the hottest models in the country, one of the best paid and best known. You could be meeting anyone you wanted to meet—movie stars, politicians, hell—I don't know. It seems you live like a recluse."

"Oh, Harold," I laughed. "I'm just busy."

Anita interrupted. "You really should relax a little more, Diane," she said, with big-sisterly concern.

I looked from one to the other. "Do you think I'm screwing up in some way?"

"Well," said Harold, "actually, it wouldn't hurt

for you to be a little more social. It wouldn't hurt your career, that is. There're a lot of people who'd like to meet you, people who are important in the business."

I threw up my hands. "What are you getting at, Harold?"

"Well. . . ." He looked at Anita.

She said, "We'd like to give you a party."

"What?"

"A party. It'd be a good chance to thank a lot of people who've helped you along, and make new friends and, well, it's just generally good PR."

I was curiously embarrassed. "What kind of party? I mean, what excuse would you use for a party? Birthday?"

"No," said Harold decisively, "the less said about birthdays the better."

"We were thinking," said Anita, "about a sort of thank-you party."

I looked at her blankly.

"You know," she continued, "thanking all the people who've helped you. The advertising agencies, photographers . . . and kind of spice the whole thing up with celebrities."

"I don't know any celebrities."

"You can if you want to. All we have to do is invite them. That's what we mean. You should use your success, enjoy it. We can get anyone you want to a party for you," said Harold.

"I'm flabbergasted," I said, laughing nervously. "But I really don't know how to go about giving a party."

Both Harold and Anita smiled. "We know how

to give a party," Harold said. "Leave everything to us. All we wanted from you was your agreement. And, of course, your presence."

"Well," I said flippantly, "I guess I can work you in some evening."

That was the origin of the affair held at the Panther, a new disco under a warehouse in SoHo, which was written up on women's pages and in people columns all across the country. Everyone was there: politicians, actors, writers, journalists, other models, and even an old astronaut, whom nobody recognized.

I wandered through the evening feeling as though a spotlight was on me. Harold and Anita had been right: the party was terrific PR. However, it wasn't really much fun—at least not for me. It was out and out work. A lot of the East Coast Bin-Bin Bead people were there and even some of the West Coast cadre (Mr. Duplessis had regretfully declined, but sent a centerpiece of 120 long-stemmed roses, which looked as though he had stripped every bush in California). I had called William myself to invite him, but he couldn't get away. "I'd give anything to be there, Diane," he said. "Both Helen and I are so damned disappointed we can't make it. But I've got to be in court the next morning at nine o'clock, and there's no way I can swing the trip."

I hadn't really expected him to come. "I'll tell you all about it," I said cheerfully.

Others from my past did appear. At one point I found myself introducing Barry Boston to Raymond Horn. I had not worked much with Barry after my first year, but I'd always remembered the evening I sat on a stool in red gauze, feeling like a bumpkin, as he and Cissie performed on a pile of vividly colored rags. I would have liked to invite Cissie, too, but no one knew what had happened to her, least of all Barry, who looked blank when I mentioned her name. His date for my party was a girl who couldn't have been more than twelve years old. She clung to him during the evening while he, in black silk jumpsuit and gold chains meshing with the hair on his chest, looked bored and stoned. Raymond was dashing and friendly, though the kiss he planted on my cheek in greeting betrayed not the slightest interest in getting back to his sunken tub high over Central Park. His tanned pate gleamed under the flashing strobes of the Panther's dance floor as I shrieked over the music: "Raymond, this is Barry! Barry, Raymond! I've worked with both of you!" I smiled idiotically through the deafening roar as they shook hands with barely a glance at each other. After a few minutes they drifted away.

I did manage to spend a few minutes with Mr. Mane, who came only as a courtesy to me, wearing a dark suit and a pained expression. I guided him to the VIP lounge where the sound, though by no means blocked out, was somewhat curtailed, and though we still had to raise our voices, we didn't have to scream in order to be heard.

"It's a very nice party," said Mr. Mane unconvincingly.

"It's so good of you to come. I'm flattered you took the trouble."

He patted my hand. "How's work going?"

I knew he was talking about photography. "I'm

having trouble getting assignments, especially since. . . ."

I had only to gesture for him to understand. "Well," he said philosophically, "you'll just have to keep trying." Then, smiling, he patted my hand again. "You're good, and you'll get ahead." As far as he was concerned the Bin-Bin Bead Girl didn't exist, and I was grateful for his ignoring her. He left shortly afterwards. I escorted him to the door, and though several people I didn't know flashed smiles at me and a few photographers from the papers called me to look at them, no one appeared to recognize him. He was not bothered by the crowd's indifference.

Later I saw Angela and Rena dancing with two young men so perfectly symmetrical and golden that they had to be gay; the four of them shimmered to the music under the pulsing lights, forming and re-forming partnerships that, because of their movements and expressions, couldn't help but be erotic. They created a space for themselves as Rena and one boy would bump asses while Angela and the other would rub shoulders, then the couples would converge and separate into different combinations as smoothly as a carefully twisted kaleidoscopic design. I watched them, fascinated and envious, though of precisely what I couldn't say: their apparently total and mindless involvement in that particular moment, I suppose.

I couldn't indulge myself in such an escape at my own party. I had to greet and introduce and smile and pose and dance and smile and flatter and cajole and smile. I buttered up the Bin-Bin Bead people from the coast even while tracking down art directors and letting them know I would love to shoot a layout now that I had some free time. I shook the hands of every city politician from the mayor down to some fat city council member from Staten Island. I showed the governor's date where the ladies' room was and signed an autograph for the daughter of a television soap opera star I'd never heard of. Harold or Anita or the Bin-Bin executives kept dragging people to me with bright smiles and eager introductions: "Oh, Diane, here's a fan of yours," one or the other would yell as they propelled some new body into view and I grasped his or her hand with a sincere clasp and a very warm smile. The noise was so ferocious that we were reduced to shouting catch phrases and buzz words at each other, and I suppose that was just as well. At least it was less of a strain for me.

By four o'clock, I was both high on my own adrenalin and exhausted, and the party showed no signs of letting up. There were more people than ever, because the doormen were letting in a lot of the general public who'd been standing sheeplike at the entrance for hours, waiting for a chance to mingle with the beautiful people within. I wanted to go home but felt it would be rude. Also, I didn't want to go home alone. I'd come with Harold, but it seemed to me that surely I'd meet some terrific guy at my own party—some fantasy figure who didn't have anything to do with modeling or photography or junk jewelry. Harry Ort III walked by and I had a fleeting moment of desire to visit his game room, but even as he waved a greeting he was joined by a beautiful young girl whose picture I had seen on hair-dye ads. There were plenty of other men around, many unattached, it seemed, but either they were gay or intimidated, or possibly just not interested. I had become a wallflower at my own party. Finally, at five o'clock, I slipped out after telling Harold I was leaving.

"I hope you had a good time, Diane," he shouted into my ear.

"Great," I screamed back. "Just great. Thanks. Talk to you tomorrow."

I got a cab and rode home through patches of steam rising from the streets, as a cold city dawn began to illuminate the outlines of buildings that kept growing taller as we sped unimpeded uptown.

The party, from everybody else's point of view, was a grand success. There was reams of publicity for me, the Harold Ames Agency and Bin-Bin Beads; tremendous good will, according to Harold, was created among photographers and art directors the agency had to deal with; and I had further burnished my image. I suppose that the party was also valuable to me in a very personal way. It showed I hadn't been missing a thing by giving up the disco-bar-supper club scene. I had never really felt deprived, and now I knew that if I found a party that was given for me dull, I'd probably go out of my mind with boredom at those given for someone else. Consequently, with every bit of spare time the Bin-Bin people gave me, I plunged into photography without one regretful glance at what I might be missing by way of fun. It was as though the party had been given to show me that whatever fulfillment

I might achieve did not lie in that direction, but rather in work. Good old work ethic.

But if fashion magazines had been wary of me before, they were extremely cautious now about throwing work my way. Neither they nor advertisers could take me very seriously as a photographer after seeing pictures of me discoing, hair and beads flying with apparent abandon. There was too much at stake for them to risk giving a shoot to an amateur or a dilettante, and even my growing body of work didn't overcome their reluctance. I did get a few jobs, but they were small and widely spaced.

In order to keep working with a camera, I had to rely more and more on the skin mags. I began to branch out and get in touch with a few of the raunchier ones.

That's how I got the assignment from *Horny Nights*, whose content was as straightforward as its title. The magazine specialized in photographed adult comic strips, telling rudimentary stories that always led to orgasmic conclusions. The plots were streamlined: for example, a burly man in overalls walks into a room where a half-naked woman is sprawled on the couch and the ballooned caption is something like, "Hello, ma'am, I'm here to fix your pipes." In the next two or three pages they go at it in every way possible. As simple as that.

Every month one of the features was a double-spread orgy sequence, showing various combinations culminating in a free-for-all. I agreed to do it if the magazine would furnish the models. Like editors on most skin mags, the staff of *Horny Nights* wanted as little work to do as possible, and they usually insisted that the photographer furnish and pay for the models. I told them I couldn't round up the three men and one woman quickly enough to meet their deadline. I caught them in a bind, so they grudgingly took responsibility for assembling the cast.

I was apprehensive on the morning of the shoot, as I waited in my downtown studio, because I'd never done such explicit group work before, and I didn't have much faith in the ability of the magazine to assemble particularly appealing models. I was reassured on the last count as the models began to arrive. There are an awful lot of handsome, pretty people in New York who need money.

The first to check in was a tall, thin man with a shy grin and longish blond hair. He was wearing a down vest, flannel shirt and blue jeans, and introduced himself in a pleasant Midwestern voice as Joe Bayliss. I guessed he was in his early twenties and probably an actor (I was right on both scores). The next arrival was a shorter, stockier man in his early thirties, with dark, wavy, receding hair and full sensual lips. Dressed in a tie and sports jacket, he said his name was Vince Carleton. Helen Briggs, the only female, came next. She was in her late twenties, a blonde, blue-eyed Nordic type with a pleasant face and beautiful teeth. She removed her down coat to reveal what was probably a nice figure under the blue jeans and turtleneck sweater. She was friendly and unabashed as she shook my hand. "Gosh," she said, "I'd heard the photographer was a woman but I didn't believe it. Nice to meet you. Glad I won't be alone." I liked her immediately; she was so matter-of-fact and natural. She nodded to Joe and Vince, took a container of coffee from a brown sack and opened it. "Missed breakfast," she said cheerfully.

"I should get a coffee pot in here, but I keep forgetting," I answered. Joe smiled and dropped his eyes as Vince looked closely at me. I could tell he thought he recognized me, but wasn't quite sure.

A few minutes later, Ben Drake completed the group. He was about thirty, tall, with close-cut brown hair and a mustache that framed his mouth like parentheses. He was wearing a grey business suit under his navy blue topcoat. "I've got an appointment later this afternoon and didn't want to go home to change," he said, apologizing for his clothes. He quickly removed the coat, jacket and tie and hung them on the rack. He was nervous and watchful, and nodded to the others warily as he gingerly took his seat on the couch next to Helen.

They all looked at me expectantly. I felt like the new teacher on the first day of school, standing before the class in my Ralph Lauren tweed skirt and ecru silk blouse. I had taken particular care to appear businesslike and groomed.

"I guess we're all here," I said with chirpy good humor. "I think we can get started. I suppose they told you at the magazine to bring your own makeup?"

Everyone except Ben nodded. He looked abashed. "Makeup? Gee, I didn't know anything about make-up. I don't have any. Should I go get some? Where could I go?" He was much more worried than the situation called for.

"I don't think you'll need very much, if any at all," I said reassuringly. "Maybe a little powder later on to keep down the shine. Perhaps someone else can loan you a base."

"Sure," said Vince. "Be glad to."

"I don't know how to put it on." Ben was nervous.

"Nothing to it," said Vince drily. He began to undress, neatly hanging his jacket, then his slacks, then draping his tie and shirt on top of both. He stood in jockey shorts and socks, revealing a broad chest with thick black hair and sturdy legs, equally hirsute.

Joe slipped out of his Levis, shirt and underwear, and within a minute stood stark naked. His tall, thin body was without any hair except at his crotch and armpits. His cock was large and circumcised, and dangled in front of a relatively small set of balls. He kept a shy, private smile in place as he stood next to the clothes rack, waiting for instructions.

Helen set her coffee aside and slipped off her sweater while still sitting down. Her breasts, encased in a white bra, were full and large. She stood, and I could see, as she unzipped her blue jeans and stepped out of them, that her waist tapered prettily before flaring into full hips. "I thought I'd just use a base and some lipstick," she said casually. "That OK?"

"I think so," I said. "Although maybe a little blue eyeshadow, if you have it."

She nodded. "Yeah, sure." She opened her make-up kit and set to work.

From the corner of my eye I could see Ben watching the others with a half-open mouth and scared eyes. He continued to sit, huddled like a refugee, while the others, with various degrees of unconcern, went about getting ready for the camera. In an effort to put him at ease I said, low enough so that no one else could hear, "Is this your first shoot?"

Apprehension, then caution flashed across his face in quick succession, and he answered, "Well, I've done some camera work, but not exactly this type." He stood. His reply was pure bluster and meant nothing beyond confirming that he was definitely an amateur. That didn't bother me too much. He was good looking and seemed to have a solid body; with three pros, one neophyte wouldn't be such a drawback. All in all, I had lucked into a better crowd than I'd expected.

Ben began to undress with exaggerated casualness. He even swaggered a bit as he unbuttoned his shirt and hung it up, then sat and removed his shoes and socks. But when he had to remove his pants he turned his back to the room and slipped out of them, revealing good, well-developed legs and a nice ass through white boxer shorts.

Joe lit a joint and, with his shy smile, passed it to him. Ben looked worriedly over his shoulder at me, as though for permission, then took the joint and inhaled gratefully. Still, however, he kept his back to the room. I pretended not to notice, but I wondered what he was hiding.

Vince was skillfully putting a thin coating of powder over his forehead as Joe wandered over to him, holding out the joint. Vince took it with a smile of thanks and inhaled deeply, retaining the smoke as he went back to work stroking make-up on his cheeks. Helen was equally nonchalant. "Thanks, hon," she said to Joe as he offered her the grass and expertly sucked in a deep lungful.

Joe came to me a little diffidently, as though he were not quite sure of the protocol. I was almost tempted to fake it, but I decided I probably couldn't fool them, so I smiled broadly—almost laughed—and said, "Think I'll have to pass. After all, I've got to do the work while all of you have the fun."

The joke was weak, but they laughed dutifully and we all felt a little more of a group. The toke had given Ben courage enough to face the rest of us and even though he held his hands in front of him I could see why he had been so timid. Unlike the other men he was sporting an enormous erection which strained against his boxer shorts. The poor guy was embarrassed to have a hard-on. He quickly resumed his seat on the couch, crossed his legs, and stared straight ahead. The others pretended not to notice.

After Vince had finished his make-up, he asked Ben, kindly, "Do you want me to touch you up?"

Ben flashed a look at me. "I don't know."

"Why don't you just do his forehead," I said. Like Vince, Ben had a hairy chest that probably wouldn't glare. With his smooth torso, Joe had had to touch up his pectorals and arms as well as his face. As Ben stoically shut his eyes, Vince sat next to him and dabbed powder over his face.

Helen completed her make-up. "Unsnap me, hon, will you?" she asked Joe, who leaned over and undid the catch of her bra. Her breasts drooped but did not sag. She powdered them quickly. "Is this in color or black and white?" she asked me.

Before I could answer, Vince said, "Huh! for *Horny Nights*? The only thing they put in color are the centerfolds."

"Well, then," said Helen, "I won't put any rouge on my nipples." The statement had the practical sing-song ring of experience. She quickly drew a comb through her long blonde hair.

It had taken them less than half an hour since they had arrived to get ready for the camera. I thought that if this were a fashion shoot, we would just now probably be sending down for coffee and no one would expect the actual shoot to begin for another three hours. In this case, within three hours we'd all be finished and on to whatever other duties our lives had in store for us.

"I believe we're ready," I said.

Vince and Helen stepped out of their underwear and tossed their garments to the clothes stand. Ben looked around desperately, then clenched his jaw and whipped off his shorts. His cock sprang up from his groin, large and rigid. The poor guy was as hot as a pistol and humiliated, but he kept his expression neutral. The others still pretended not to notice anything.

I had already set up the photographic area. There was a couch with a paisley throw, a table with a dildo and vibrator on it, and a chair. *Horny Nights*, unlike most other skin mags, did not go in for fantasy settings (such as Swiss chalets or medieval taverns) or semi-costumes (policewomen were popular that season). No, the unvarnished instructions from the art director summed up the requirements: "All we want is cock and cunt, a little tit and less ass." The setting obviously was unimportant.

"OK, Helen," I said brightly, "you sit on the couch, right in the center, and Joe, you kneel on the couch beside her. That's right. Vince, go to the other side and lean over Helen's breast . . . more to the side, I want to show your mouth open over the nipple, but not touching it . . . uh huh . . . and Ben," I was careful to keep my tone of voice cheerful and, I hoped, comforting, "you kneel with your back to me between Helen's legs—that's right. Helen, spread your legs more and take Joe and Vince's cocks in your hands. Um . . . Ben, bring your face up closer to Helen's pussy, but don't touch it yet. Just open your mouth as though you were going to take a bite of it."

Ben was fiery red, whether from desire or embarrassment I couldn't tell. His eyes had a hunted look. The others were alert, attentive and quite calm as they carried out my instructions. Helen grasped the two cocks—Joe's was truly enormous, and Vince's was thick and uncut; both were soft—indifferently as though they were subway straps, and looked at me for further guidance. Joe and Vince kept their eyes on me questioningly. Ben hovered over Helen's pussy—which was neatly covered by blonde hair, sparse enough to allow the tender pink of the skin to show through—as though he were in a coma. He seemed to be having trouble breathing.

"OK, everyone, get ready," I said. "Here we go."

Instantly Helen rolled her eyes up and pursed her lips as though transported by pleasure. Vince shot his tongue toward her nipple and Joe threw back his head and closed his eyes in ecstasy. Only Ben remained exactly as he was, with his open mouth and frightened eyes, he looked as though Helen's pussy had somehow fatally shot him.

I lowered the camera. "Ben," I said gently, "why don't you close your eyes. . . ."

He squeezed them shut, which only heightened the impression that he was in extreme pain.

I walked over to him, turned his head a little more toward Helen's crotch and said, "Now, just relax. Don't squint. That's better. Don't hold your mouth so widely open. That's better. Much better. Now, just keep it that way." I walked back to focus and said, "OK, here we go." They all resumed their poses as I clicked.

Ben jumped, obviously unaccustomed to the strobe flash. I had not done a Polaroid test shot, so he hadn't known what to expect. "Let's do that one again," I said gaily. "Exactly the same. That's right." This time as I pressed the shutter and the umbrella lights flashed, everyone held the pose. I shot a couple more with minor changes, then went to the next pose.

There was no story, no development: all I had to deliver were plenty of shots of Helen's pussy and the men's cocks. The cocks didn't have to be hard, and usually weren't in the pages of *Horny Nights*. I suppose, because the budgets of the photographers were so stringent, they didn't have enough time to coax erections out of their models. On that score, I could certainly have given the readers a little bonus because Ben managed to stay hard well into the middle of the session. I didn't want to show his erection, though, because it would make Joe and Vince look like pikers. I wanted to try for an all-hard shot, but decided to wait until the end of the session to see if there was enough time to get the men in the proper mood.

"That's good," I said cheerily. "Now, Helen, stretch out on the couch, with your head on the armrest . . . um hum . . . and Vince you crouch over her with cock near her mouth. That's right. Great. Joe, go and kneel between Helen's legs and aim your cock at her pussy, as though you were just ready to put it in . . . good. Ben, you kneel on the side and put your mouth over Helen's nipple. Turn your head so we can see your tongue. That's good."

"OK everybody, get ready . . . uh . . . Ben, just close your eyes slightly—no, don't screw them up—just lightly . . . that's right, and make your mouth a little less rigid . . . no, keep your tongue out. That's perfect, now hold that. OK, everybody. . . ." Helen opened her mouth in a silent gasp, and Vince, holding his cock near her mouth, wrenched his head to one side and closed his eyes. Joe held his huge cock just above Helen's pussy, his chin drawn into his chest as though pleasure had contracted all his muscles. I took several shots.

Sweat was pouring off Ben in rivulets. His broad shoulders were glistening and his face shone as though he had been jogging at high noon in August. This might have been OK, if the others had not remained so dry and cool-looking. Rather than oil them up, I decided to dry Ben off.

"Let's take a break," I said, while getting a towel. "Ben, could you come over here?" I asked pleasantly, being careful not to make a fuss. Softly, so only he could hear, I said, "I think you're going to need a little more powder, and maybe some on your shoulders." He stood in front of me, embarrassed. "Let me dry off your shoulders." Dutifully, he turned as though he had put himself entirely in my hands. He still had an erection, though it was not as stiff as earlier. I patted him dry and called, "Vince? Could we use a little more of your make-up?"

"Sure," said Vince, walking over with the case in his extended hand. He stood near me as I dabbed the powder over Ben's shoulders. At first I didn't pay much attention to Vince, but soon I noticed that his arm—muscular and covered with black hair—brushed against mine several times. Surprised, I glanced quickly at his face, which was inscrutable.

"That should do it," I said cheerily, as I returned the make-up to Vince. He met my eyes with a smile that was half polite and half questioning, and very brief. Slight though the message was, it was sufficiently potent to work its way into a chamber of my imagination and begin to ferment. Consciously, however, I put the whole exchange out of my mind as I called my cast back to work.

"Now then, let's get started," I said briskly, looking at my watch. We had worked only about forty-five minutes and I had already shot about half the needed pictures. "Helen, sit on the couch with your left leg over the back and your right foot on the floor—a good spread of the legs. That's right. Now, Joe, you take the dildo there and hold it at her ass while you point your cock at her pussy. Good . . . very good. Let's see now, Vince. You straddle Helen's chest, with your cock over her mouth and reach behind and take her nipple in your fingers . . . yes . . . except move a little closer to her mouth. That's right. Ben, stand behind the couch and lean over and take Helen's other nipple in your fingers. Put your other hand on her knee, as though you were helping spread her legs. Good. OK, now, get ready."

Helen opened her mouth and narrowed her eyes, as though she were about to pass out from the excitement. Vince threw back his head and grimaced, his eyes closed. Joe gritted his teeth and curled his lips and looked meanly at Helen's pussy. Ben gazed painfully straight into the camera.

"Ben," I said, "look down at the nipple. With anticipation. Purse your lips as though you wanted to put it in your mouth. Lean more toward it. That's right. Now, everybody, here we go. Hold it." I took several shots, then rearranged them into three poses more before I finally got enough film to fill out the assignment.

I checked my watch and found I had brought everything in an hour under the time I had allowed. I decided to go for the hard-on shot, if the men were willing. It was a delicate proposition, because, for all I knew, neither Vince nor Joe was able to get it up. There was, of course, no question about Ben.

"I'd like," I said carefully, "to give a little something extra to this layout." They looked at me expectantly. "I think it might be really hot, for example, if Helen spread her pussy to show even more pink than she has and . . . you know it might be really great if you guys all got it up and stood over her . . ." I added the last as though it had just occurred to me.

"You mean you want a hard-on shot?" asked Vince neutrally.

"Yeah, that might be hot." I looked at the three men, trying to search out resistance. I couldn't discern any, so I said, "Let's give it a try."

Helen inserted her fingers in her pussy, looked at it critically. Joc lit another joint and stared dreamily at the ceiling as he passed it to Helen, while he held his cock in his hand and played with it, squeezing it and running his thumb along the shaft. Vince spit on his hand, smoothed back his foreskin and lightly massaged his glans. Ben watched the others, fascinated, but not touching his own cock, which had finally gone limp and lay along his inner thigh like a convalescent snake. He caught my eye and shamefacedly reached down and took his cock in hand.

As Helen played with her pussy her nipples got larger and stood up, and her face flushed. Joe, courteously, with a shy smile, reached over and took one between his thumb and forefinger. His cock was hard and huge, and, as though responding to an amenity, Helen took its base gently in her fist. She and Joe smiled at each other, and Helen coquettishly kissed the air in his direction with a liquid smack of her lips. Joe laughed.

Vince, his cock hard, watched me covertly with

sidelong glances. He knelt on the sofa, a little apart from Joe and Helen, massaging his cock, making his large balls sway back and forth with the motion. He was breathing through half-opened lips, and his chest, with its haze of black curly hair, rose and fell rapidly. As I watched him, and became aware of his eyes on me, I felt a warm rush in my thighs.

Ben revived his erection so quickly he might have snapped a switch that unleashed a sexual current. His cock stood from his brown pubic hair as red and throbbing as it had been when he undressed. Now, however, he had lost his embarrassment, since everyone was doing it, and he looked from Helen to me with an expression very like satisfaction. At the same time, there was a spark of something more in his eye as his gaze roamed between us. I found myself wondering what his cock would feel like, and whether the taut skin around his narrow waist would be hard to the touch. I caught myself breathing through my mouth and quickly closed it, clamping my jaws as though to bite the head off desire.

"That's good," I said primly, keeping my voice light and cheerful. "Helen, you stay right in the middle and spread your legs. Use both hands to open your pussy—that's right." She had pulled the outer lips of her pussy to reveal the gleaming pink inner lips, which crinkled moistly like the petals of an exotic flower. She probed shallowly, and agitated her finger in the spot where her clitoris must have been. A look of thoughtful self-involvement showed on her face.

Joe watched her, both his hands on her

nipples, lightly brushing them, pinching, twisting as though they were dials on a TV set. I felt my own nipples grow stiff.

"Joe, I think you can stay as you are. Maybe move a little closer. That's right."

Vince was still on his knees on the sofa, his cock hard, its wet, red tip now fully released from the foreskin. As he played with it he kept his eyes, but not his head, turned toward me.

"I think, Vince," I said, after clearing my throat, "that you can throw one leg over the back of the sofa, and move closer to Helen's mouth. Just straddle the sofa . . . that's right. Keep your balls on this side, toward the camera."

The studio seemed much warmer. Without thinking, I unbuttoned the top couple buttons of my blouse and fanned myself with the loose material. Vince turned to look directly at me and I felt the heat of a blush cross my face.

Ben was unabashedly looking at Helen's pussy. His cock was so taut and pulsing that I thought he might shoot off without further provocation.

"Ben, you crouch on the floor at Helen's feet. Put your left leg down a little so we can see your cock. Further . . . that's right. Now lean your cheek against her thigh, and aim your mouth at her pussy. That's right. That's very good." I surveyed the tableau and found it hot. I was going to have to give very few directions because everybody was now into what he and she were supposed to be doing. Fantasy had for a few moments become welded with reality. "Get ready," I said, raising my camera, and getting the scene into focus. Helen lost a little of her look of reverie, and Vince turned his head from me to her, and that was the extent of the transformation. "Here we go." I snapped several pictures, having them slightly alter their positions—move a little closer, open a little wider—but keeping the same general setup. The four of them appeared to grow hotter as I snapped away. I know I did. By the time I was finished with the roll of film I was breathing more rapidly and my pussy was moist and yearning. Ruefully, I glanced at the vibrator on the table, thinking I'd go for it as soon as the studio cleared out.

"That does it, kids," I said, plastering forced good humor over my desire. "You've been a swell crew." I smiled brightly.

For an instant, I thought they hadn't heard me. Then Helen stuck our her tongue and tickled the red head of Vince's cock. It was meant, I think, to be a playful gesture, but somewhere between the intention and the execution, sensuality triumphed, and she took it into her mouth. Vince drew in his breath and put his hand on her head. In that instant he turned to me, his black eyes intense with invitation.

I stood dangling the camera by my side, both wanting to join the scene and yet not willing to relinquish my control of the group. I was nervous about gossip. True, I was hardly celibate, but screwing one on one, or even one on two as with Angela and Rena (although that really wouldn't count, I thought) was a different proposition from joining a group. A group was an orgy, and orgies could generate some nasty talk.

But I was hot.

Joe rubbed the tip of his enormous cock

against Helen's shoulder, like a puppy scratching for attention, and she turned from Vince and took it in her mouth. Ben watched from the floor, his face upturned between Helen's thighs with the same sort of expression children have while watching their first circus. He moved nearer Helen's pussy and tentatively, as though he were afraid of being burned, stuck out his tongue and licked its edges. She squirmed and shoved it toward him.

I put the camera down. Vince was staring at me so insistently that I had to acknowledge him, so I dropped any pretense of indifference and met his eyes. Wordlessly he held out his hand, while with the other he supported his cock as though he were taming it. I hesitated. He didn't move or change his expression. I took the four or so steps toward the couch and Vince circled my waist and pulled me close to him, and kissed me with his mouth open.

As his tongue sought mine, he unbuttoned my blouse and unfastened the snap on my skirt so expertly that it was obvious I was not the first woman he had ever undressed. He unsnapped my bra and pulled down my half slip and pantyhose, all the while keeping his tongue in my mouth. I had taken his face between my hands, and ran my fingers through his hair, as his kiss attached me to him like a magnet. He began to play with my breasts, gently stroking them, then grasped the nipples and brought pressure with his fingernails. I felt another hand move up my inner thigh and grasp my crotch, cupping and rubbing my pussy. Suddenly I felt a full head of hair against the same tender skin and there was hot breath against my pussy. A mouth began to burrow into my crotch; I surmised it was Ben, and raised my right leg to allow him full access.

Out of habit, I had kept my eyes closed as Vince and I kissed. I opened them when he lowered his head to take a nipple between his teeth, and saw that Helen had somehow managed to swallow more than half Joe's cock down her throat. I remember marveling at her ability, even as my body was electrified by the sensations generated by the two mouths at work on it.

Vince moved lower, to my navel, then down, pushing Ben away from my pussy so that he could taste it himself. Ben stood behind me and rubbed his cock over my ass, then prodded experimentally with head. I moaned and spread my legs, as my knees sank to the couch. Vince moved up until he was sitting on the cushion, and I lowered my pussy to where I thought his cock was. I was right on target, and he filled me so deliciously that I groaned and wrapped my arms around his neck. As I began to move up and down on him, using my knees as levers, Ben continued playing with my anus, inserting a finger and wiggling it a little, then following with his cock. He was standing between my and Vince's legs, determined to penetrate.

Helen was still sucking on Joe. She had inserted the vibrator into her pussy and was barely agitating it as she moved even farther up on his cock. Joe leaned across her and, with a surprising sweetness under the circumstances, kissed me chastely on the lips: it was the sort of kiss that, in a more innocent age, one might expect on a first date. I was so astonished that I half gasped, half laughed. At that moment, Ben entered my ass.

I had not been fucked in the ass since the night in the playroom of Harry Ort III. As Ben inched his way through my sphincter, I at first wanted to stop him. But the pleasure increased as my asshole became not accustomed, but accommodating to Ben's cock. Strangely enough, one of the thoughts that flitted through my head was, "This isn't proper." But rather than intimidate, the idea seemed to quell whatever inhibitions remained, for I thrust downward, impaling myself farther on the cocks of Vince and Ben. That instant was one of the most cxciting I've ever experienced.

Helen at that moment moaned, sobbed, then jerked her head from Joe's cock as she screamed. With the vibrator she had reached an orgasm that, momentarily, at least, devastated her. Joe kept his hands on her breasts as she writhed and stiffened. Then he took his glistening cock in hand and began, philosophically, to work on it himself. I reached across the prone form of Helen, cupped his ass with my hand, and pulled him near me. He was surprised and caught off balance, and had to support himself on the back of the couch to keep from falling. I took his cock in my mouth and found the taste enormously satisfying.

I sucked as I moved up and down, working the three cocks. I have never been so given over to sheer gratification; yet my mind, like a stormy lake, kept tossing up perceptions. I remember something I had read about the Byzantine Empress Theodosia, who said it was her desire to have all her orifices filled, and preferably simultaneously. There I was, like a Byzantine Empress, being stuffed from every direction. Theodosia was considered depraved. I thought of myself as liberated. I licked and sucked and swallowed Joe's cock, and strained to bring Vince's as deeply into my pussy as it would go. At the same time I pushed against Ben who had stood like a wall behind me, swiveling his way into my ass.

Joe began to whimper and grappled with my head. He held me steady as he tremblingly humped my mouth. Suddenly he groaned loudly and I felt his sperm shoot to the back of my throat. It was thick and salty, and I swallowed without a second thought.

Joe collapsed near Helen, but kept a hand on my nipple as his shy smile returned, considerably weaker. He blinked up at me like a large and satiated pet.

He continued to play with my left nipple as Vince sucked on my right one. Behind me Ben's pace accelerated, and his breath came quicker as he grabbed my ass with both hands. "Oh," he moaned, then, more loudly, "Ohhhhh." He pumped faster and faster and his thrusts became rough as he tried to get all his cock up my ass. I don't know whether he succeeded or not, but I do know he went about as far as I'd care to have anyone go. He shot off with a loud cry of, "Oh, my God! Oh, I'm coming!" He quivered like an animal that's been shot and stopped in its tracks as he grasped me so tightly he almost pulled me off Vince's cock. I worked my ass and pussy simultaneously as Ben's cock slowly pulled out and he continued to groan. As soon as he was free, he fell to his knees and kissed the cheek of my ass. He held onto my legs and feet as though they would save him from drowning.

Vince looked up at me and smiled—a slow, ironic, sensual smile—and clutched my hips. He pulled me down on his cock until we seemed permanently joined, and I took his shoulders in my hands. Holding me by the waist and keeping his cock in my pussy, he moved us both so that my back was against the sofa and he was on top. He then began to fuck in earnest, up and down, and rotated his hips so that he reamed every millimeter of my pussy. I felt the first faint tremors of an orgasm and stiffened my back, then suddenly, unable to control myself, I threw my legs around him, pulling him closer as he gyrated so violently I thought we might be knocked off the sofa.

His face hung over mine, and his lips were drawn back from his clamped teeth in an almost cruel grimace as his cock slammed into my slit. He squinted and the cords of his neck stood out; suddenly, with a surprised yell, the tension was released and I felt his cum flooding my pussy. At that moment, I exploded and pulled him to me with such violence that I knocked the breath out of myself.

The chances of a simultaneous orgasm are slim. I suppose they're increased when the ratio is three to one. Whatever the case, I've never experienced anything quite like that before or since. I lay under Vince, exhausted, sated, wonderstruck.

Helen was the first to break the silence. "That

certainly beats the *usual* coffee break," she said as she got to her feet.

We laughed—I, rather nervously—and Vince moved to allow me to sit up.

From the floor Ben, looking both surprised and pleased said, "I've never done anything like that before." It wasn't clear whether he was referring to having sex in a group or fucking me in the ass. No one asked for clarification.

I felt that something was called for from me since I was the hostess. "Neither have I," I replied graciously, "and I can't think of a nicer bunch for a first time."

"Hey, that's cool," said Joe dreamily, as he stood up and ran his fingers through my hair. "You're a real cool lady." He ambled over to the clothes rack and began to dress.

Ben got up, following Joe's example. "In fact," he said to the room at large, "I've never done *any* of this before, I mean, not even the pictures." He looked at each of us with confiding candor.

"You did very well for a beginner," I said. "On all fronts."

He blushed and modestly averted his eyes. For an embarrassed instant I thought he was going to say, "Ah, gee, it was nothing," but he controlled himself and joined Joe in silence at the clothes rack.

Vince continued to lie on the couch, his legs extended, his elbow on the armrest, his head on his hand. Helen slipped into her bra and turned for me to fasten it. I envied her complete lack of self-consciousness, because I was constrained. I could not dispel the feeling that I was responsible for what had happened, since I was the photographer, and in charge of the studio and everything that took place in it. I was not sufficiently liberated to accept our little orgy as commonplace. My uneasiness translated into prissiness as I set about dressing with a prim smile, as though I could will the occurrence out of existence if I behaved like a Connecticut matron. "I'm sorry I don't have anything to drink," I said inanely, as though the event called for refreshments. "I really must get a coffee pot and a refrigerator in here for when . . . uh . . . people come by."

Joe and Helen smiled noncommittally and Ben said, "Oh, that's OK. *I* certainly wasn't expecting anything." He still looked fazed by the experience.

Vince had not moved, but remained prone, dreamily watching the rest of us. In about three minutes, I was dressed, and I began to feel more reassured. I ran a comb through my hair, freshened my lipstick and began to assemble my cameras and the film I had used.

Helen and Joe were in their down coats and together they came over to me. "I guess we'll be shoving off," said Helen. "I'd love to have prints."

"Of course," I said, "I'll send all of you prints. You know," I continued, raising my voice so everyone could hear, "that *Horny Nights* is paying your fees?"

They murmured that, yes, they understood that, and I signed their vouchers.

Helen held out her hand. "Thanks, Diane," she said.

Joe leaned over and kissed me on the cheek.

"It was real cool. It really was." His smile was sweet and uncomplicated.

Ben was standing near the sofa, putting on his topcoat, transformed back into the conventional and diffident commuter who had arrived a few hours before. "Well," he said with a false laugh, "it sure has been an experience. I won't forget it in a hurry."

"It was nice of you to help out," I said.

"Yeah. Well, you know, I was . . . well, broke, and all. . . ."

"Happens to the best of us."

"Well, I hope my luck's going to change. I've got an interview this afternoon."

"What for?"

"With a brokerage house. I'm a stockbroker. I was just layed off last month and, you know, I thought I'd get a little cash. . . ."

"Terrific," I said. "I hope you have luck with the interview. I'll send your proofs."

"Yeah. I'd like to see them. They're for my fiancée."

"Oh?"

"Yeah. She got me the job. She works for *Horny Nights*, and thought it might be kinky to have pictures of me, you know, doing those things. . . ." He smiled embarrassedly.

"Well, congratulations . . . on the interview and the engagement."

"Thanks." He hesitated, unsure of how to depart, then shook hands with Vince and me and left.

Vince still had not dressed, and seemed rooted to the couch. I wondered whether he wanted to have sex again. I didn't. All I really wanted was to be alone. But, like a good hostess, I turned brightly to him and said, "That was quite a session."

He smiled slowly, his eyes watchful. "It meant a lot to me," he said. His voice was low and insinuating.

I countered by becoming even brighter and more chirpy. "One of the little rewards of this line of work. Other jobs offer paid vacations and medical insurance, but in our profession . . ." I gestured with an airiness I didn't feel.

He got to his feet and walked over to me. His nakedness didn't appear to bother him, but it did me because it implied an intimacy I didn't feel. He stood in front of me, then put his hands on my arms and said, "Diane, I really won't forget what just happened. It wasn't just a casual fuck for me."

"That's very sweet of you, Vince." I was not particularly touched.

"I hope it wasn't just an accident, a one-time thing."

I was at a loss. He elaborated. "I mean, I hope I can see you again."

That was what I was afraid he meant. As intense as the sexual encounter had been, and as pleasant as I had found all the participants to be, I did not want to repeat the experience with them, either as a group or singly. It was not shame or embarrassment or shyness. It was that I felt that all of us had met on the one level where we had something in common, and had merged for a brief time in the only relationship that was possible to us: an orgy. There was no point in trying to gouge something more profound from a purely fortuitous set of circumstances. I was annoyed at Vince for trying to imbue the event with significance, but took care not to show it. I didn't want to see Vince or have sex with him again. My penchant for loving someone if he could make me feel good had been eroded by too many one-night stands. As I realized this, I had a fleeting whiff of melancholy for my lost innocence, but I can't say I was overwhelmed by regret.

"It would be nice to meet again. I'm sure we'll run into each other." I might have been talking to some old high school chum instead of a naked, hairy man with whom I'd just experienced my first simultaneous orgasm.

He looked hurt, then purposeful. "I don't want to leave it to chance, Diane. I'd like to call you, take you out. Get to know you. Really know you."

I paused and erased my hostess expression. With all the tact I could muster I said, "Vince, I've got a full schedule. I'm working two jobs and I just can't make commitments now. Believe me, it's nothing personal. I like you a lot, but I can't get involved now in any way other than professionally." My little speech was disingenuous (after all, anyone, me included, can always get involved if she finds the right man) but it was also kind; I give myself credit for having behaved like an adult, and letting Vince know right off he didn't have a chance. There was a time when I probably would have strung him along.

Vince didn't see it that way. His expression was a cross between hurt and surly. "I wasn't asking you to marry me," he said. "I hoped we could have dinner, go to a show, be together. . . ."

"I'm sorry, Vince, but like I said. . . ."

"Yeah, yeah. I get you." He walked to the clothes rack. Wordlessly he dressed as I continued packing my equipment. I felt guilty, but at the same time I was rather pleased to be in control of a romance (for want of a better word) instead of having it controlled by the man. I couldn't help remembering the times when I, moon-eyed and vulnerable, had ended up waiting for the phone call that never came. As I zipped up my case I still thought that my way—being honest and open—was the kindest method of handling the matter.

Vince was dressed and had his coat on as I made a final check of the studio.

"I'm going uptown," I said, smiling. "Do you want to share a cab?"

"No thanks."

"Well, then. . . ." I stood at the door, giving him room to get by. He smiled coldly with his lips and started out. I put my hand on his arm and kissed his cheek. "So long, Vince. And thanks."

He nodded brusquely and walked out, leaving me feeling lousy. A little dash of sentimentality had strangely diluted the morning's adventure for me. I was confused as I tried to figure out whether I had gone forward or backward along the emotional scale. With a sigh I admitted I couldn't decide that then, locked the studio and went uptown to my other life.

Chapter 11

I thought of Vince Carleton on the night William called to announce he was coming East to discuss something with me. I was still tense after that day that had begun with the shoot of Randy Wrong (who, at that moment, I supposed, was jacking off to the accompaniment of God-knows-what—Debussy? The Stones? Wagner? And in some seedy little movie house around Times Square). I lay on the bed after the disturbing call, aware of but not watching the silent TV screen that projected its manic, colorful images across the little gallery of photographs on my bedroom wall, and I saw again Randy's sculpted torso, sturdy legs and round, hairy bottom, and remembered the spurt of jism as he climaxed. It's always the ones we can't have who are the most desirable.

At a time like that, it would have been convenient to be able to pick up the phone and call Vince Carleton and invite him over for a quickie. A foolish fantasy, of course, because he would never have gone for that; he wanted to conduct a courtship, and that's exactly what I didn't have time for. Nor did I really have the inclination. I liked my life, even though there were moments like the one I was going through, in which I was restless and lonely and nervous, and would have found another body beside me comforting.

But you can't import just bodies; they carry along with them emotional baggage that has to be sorted out and tagged and generally attended to. I wasn't willing to put up with that in order to have a steady, warm presence. We pay a price for everything, and the price for my independence was some lonely and frustrating stretches of time.

I squirmed on the bed, tired. The shoot with Randy had been a strain, and that afternoon, the shoe layout—with that little bitch, Bette, mouthing off—had also taken its toll. Unsummoned the image of Bert, the boy who was writhing on the floor as the foot fetishist, swam into my mind's eye. It was strange. I had hardly noticed him at the shoot, but now I could clearly see his smooth young skin stretched over defined though not bulging muscles, and his lips, which were full and sensual below large brown eyes. I suppose I had been overwhelmed by the memory of Randy Wrong, who was so spectacularly sexual looking, and I had been further distracted by the little set-to with Bette. But now the idea of Bert was pleasant and, as I dwelled on it, more than that, for I felt moist and open. Bert was another one who had gotten away—two in one day.

I wondered what I would do if the phone were to ring, as I ran my hand up and down over my pussy. I imagined the jangling bell and my picking up the receiver and saying *Hello*, and on the other end of the wire a voice (deep? light? boyish?—I couldn't remember; let's say boyish) would ask to speak to Miss Bourne. *Speaking,* I would say crisply. *This is Bert,* the voice would say (diffidently? breathlessly? boldly? Make it shyly). *I'm awfully sorry to bother you but I wonder if you found my portfolio at the studio?* I'd pleasantly reassure him, *No bother at all.* I'd continue, *I haven't found anything, but then I haven't looked. Where would you have left it?*

I rubbed the tip of my finger over my asshole and back again to my pussy, this time inserting it a little way. I felt the hot slickness of my inner lips, but avoided moving up to the clitoris so soon.

I don't know where I would have left it, Bert would say, worried. *I have a go-see tomorrow and, gee, without the portfolio. . . .* Comfortingly I'd cut in, *Don't worry. Why don't you come over and we'll look for it together?* Eagerly, he'd say, *Gee, could I? I'll be right there.*

Next thing I'd know the doorman would have announced a young man on the way up and I'd greet him in . . . jeans and halter? negligee? bikini? Make it a terrycloth robe. *Hi,* I'd say. Awkwardly he'd apologize. *Gee, I'm sorry to bother you.* He would be in a tee shirt and jeans, and his muscles would be more pronounced than I'd remembered, and there would be a big bulge in his crotch. Clutching my robe, I'd say, *Excuse my appearance. I was just getting ready for bed.* Distressed, he'd reply, *Gosh, I really am sorry, but it's so important to me.* Magnanimously, I'd say, *No trouble. I understand.*

I spread my legs and continued to excite the inside of my pussy, holding it open with one hand while three fingers of the other tickled the moist pink membrane within. I blew on my tits, first one, then the other, as I squirmed deeper into the bed.

Bert and I would walk around the studio, and my robe would gape open as I'd bend down to search under chairs and tables and soon I'd notice Bert was concentrating more on me than on the missing portfolio. The bulge in his pants would get larger and his mouth would hang open as we moved from place to place. *Would you have left it in the bedroom?* I'd ask. *Maybe,* he'd reply in a strangled voice.

Then we'd be in the bedroom and as I glanced around the room, I'd notice he was no longer making a pretense of looking at anything but me. *What is it?* I'd ask innocently. *You know,* he'd say, and step forward and pull me close to him, gluing his lips to mine, in an embrace so strong I would lose my breath.

I removed my hands from my pussy and took my nipples between thumbs and forefingers and lightly squeezed and rubbed them, feeling their hardness.

He would push me on the bed. As I fell the robe would open and he would stand over me, looking down, a sneer on his young face. *You think you can lead me on and get away with it,* he would say through clenched teeth. His chest would rise and fall as his eyes narrowed with lust. He would tear off his tee shirt, and rip open his jeans. His huge cock would spring at me like a tiger escaped from its cage, and I would suck in my breath with fright.

From the night table drawer, I took my vibrator and clicked it on. As I continued to agitate my left nipple I inserted the vibrator slowly, invading my pussy with its jiggling warmth. I spread my legs farther and raised my knees as I manipulated the pink, humming piece of plastic.

Bert would fling himself on me. *OK, you bitch,* he'd say violently, *I'm going to take you now.* He would plunge into my pussy with his huge cock and pump up and down like a madman while holding my left nipple between his teeth, but not too hard. *Oh,* he'd groan and *Ah,* I'd wail.

I let the vibrator move closer to my engorged clit. The sensation made my toes curl and my legs tremble.

Oh, I'm coming, he would moan. *I'm coming,* I'd reply. *Oh, God.* We'd buck and slam our bodies together as his sperm shot into my pussy and mingled with my love juices. From our throats would come the cries of jungle beasts and we'd roll over and over as each was drained by excruciating pleasure. Gasping, Bert would fall to my breast and kiss me tenderly on the lips.

I removed the vibrator, and let it lie beside me on the bed. Bert vanished. I sighed deeply, having demolished the tensions of the day.

One nice thing about a fantasy is that you can control it absolutely; but the unfortunate thing is that there are never any surprises. Fantasies are a lot cleaner than real life. There's hardly any emotional or physical mess, but that also has its negative obverse. If you indulge in them too frequently you become disappointed by and intolerant of the idiosyncrasies and peccadilloes of flesh-and-blood partners. As I lay getting my breath back, I wondered whether I would have liked to have an aftermath to my little fantasy. I decided that no, at least not with anyone I knew—not with Vince Carleton or the half-dozen or so other casual partners who might have been available to me. I might have enjoyed post-coital pillow talk with Bert, but only as I imagined him, and probably not as he really was. The problem was academic, since I was obviously fated to sleep alone that night, and just as well, because the next day I had to model in a print layout for Bin-Bin Beads.

I cleared my head of Randy Wrong and ominous hints from William, set-tos with difficult models, hard to catch photographic assignments. After washing off the vibrator, I turned down the bed and glanced around at the photographs on my wall—the gorilla, several of me, a tree in Central Park—then switched off the television set and got between the sheets. Within moments I was asleep.

The night did not entirely dispel my uneasiness. I awoke with a residue of disquietude about William's call. All other concerns of the day before had receded, washed out by the tide of sleep, but William's call, a bulky piece of flotsam, remained all too visible on the beach. As I did my warm-ups and calisthenics, ate breakfast (an apple, an orange, and granola) with the *Times*, washed my hair and took a shower, put on my jeans and sweater, and covered my head with a huge scarf—through all these motions—I kept hearing not William's words, which were unexceptional, but his tone of voice, which had alerted me.

I got to the studio five minutes before nine and was greeted by George Prentiss, the photographer who was doing the Bin-Bin layouts, with an affectionate kiss on the cheek. Iris, the make-up and hair girl (she was about fifty) also gave me a motherly kiss, and got started right away on my make-up. Now that I was an established name, my treatment was different from the first years: assistants were deferential, photographers asked me politely to be ready at such and such a time and the executives from Wade and Thomas made it a point to cossett me.

"Can I get you anything, Diane?" asked one of the minor executives from the agency.

"Thanks, Richard," I said with a big smile. I'd taken pains to learn his name. "Nothing. How are you?"

His face lit up as he told me, "Fine."

"That's good," I said, a Lady Bountiful dispensing graciousness. It wasn't phony. I really did like most of the people I worked with.

By eleven o'clock I was made up and my hair was brushed out. We were doing a series of pictures showing the range of Bin-Bin Beads ("From town to country, from shore to mountain, from split-level to skyscraper, Bin-Bin Beads *beautify*!") and for my first shot I wore a white ballgown with long gloves. Dripping rhinestones from earrings, bracelets and necklace, I glittered like a dew-covered rose. I was pleased with myself as I pranced and turned, making the skirt swirl and the jewelry coruscate under the lights. George called out directions, his voice growing more animated as he established rapport between his camera and me, and I caught his fire. My eyes gleamed and my smile sparkled. I soared on the focus of the camera, but crashed to earth when Holland Burns, the senior New York executive in charge of the Bin-Bin account interrupted. "George! Can I see you a minute?"

They conferred in whispers, looking at me, but not speaking loudly enough for me to hear. Holland called Iris over, and she, too, darted an appraising glance at me.

"What is it?" I asked. "What's the matter?" I stood on the white backdrop paper, as my energy drained from me like melting snow.

Richard, the minor executive, hurried over. "It's nothing, Diane. We—Holland—thought maybe the make-up wasn't quite right. . . ."

"What's wrong with it?" My hand flew to my face.

"Nothing. Just an idea Holland had . . ." His voice tapered off, the diminishing sound of the underling not wanting to say too much.

"What's wrong?" I repeated this louder, staring at the group conferring out of earshot.

George, looking annoyed, walked over. "Holland thinks the make-up is a little too strong."

Holland, less diplomatic, said self-importantly, "It's too harsh. It makes you look too old and hard." He turned to Iris. "Can't she be made a little more *jeune fille*?" He was a prissy, fat man in his early forties with whom I'd always gotten along.

Iris, her face impassive, said, "I can lighten the eyeshadow and tone down the lips."

"Yeah," said Holland, looking at me, his hand on his chin, "that might do it." Then, smiling at me, he said, "We'll fix you up in no time," and returned to his canvas chair at the side of the studio.

My euphoria collapsed. Though I recognized that Holland Burns was exercising one of his petty prerogatives, and that his criticism was not meant personally or spitefully (nor, even, for that matter, was it to be taken seriously) I was nonetheless dashed. I was unable to separate my appearance, or even my make-up, from myself, and any criticism, no matter how foolish and self-serving, ate at my confidence like acid. All Holland Burns wanted to do was to establish that he was in charge, and I was his means to that end. I doubt he was even aware of how disruptive his action was. I don't think he noticed that George had grown surly, Iris had crimped her lips, and I had been deflated, my ebullience squeezed out of me.

My make-up was retouched. It was all but impossible to tell the difference, and we started again. George worked heroically to get me back up to pitch, and I tried to fall in with him, to continue the magical dance we had performed before the interruption. But it was no good. I could not respond as before, partly because there was too much annoyance in George's directions—not annoyance directed against me, but annoyance just the same. Finally he called for a lunch break.

"I'm sorry, George," I said softly.

He was a blond, short, burr-headed gay man with a mustache, whose lover, a humpy Sicilian bandit type, was his principal assistant.

"Don't sweat about it, babe," he said, his arm around my waist. "It's not your fault."

But I felt it was my fault. I was the model, the object being photographed, and if I couldn't perform, the session was a failure. Holland Burns, instead of having lunch sent in, was going out. As he passed me he beamed and said, "Great work, Diane. Just great."

The asshole didn't realize how he had wrecked the shoot, the way an ignorant, uncouth child might nonchalantly smash a Fabergé egg. I was angry; partly at him, though of course I didn't show it, but mostly at myself, for not being able to handle the situation. Holland's criticism was not any worse—was, in fact, much milder—than a lot I'd been subjected to.

I was dismayed at the realization that no matter how far I got as a model—and it seemed unlikely I would get much further than I was now—I'd always be buffeted by any adverse word. A critical look, a negative opinion, even a fatuous remark about my make-up would be enough to summon my old insecurity, as paralyzing and painful as poison gas.

I had another flash. I never suffered the same feeling of inadequacy when I was on the other side of the camera, when I was focusing instead of being focused on, in spite of being responsible for much more as a photographer than as a model. As a model, I had only to appear to be what other people wanted me to be; as a photographer I was in charge of the whole works. Yet, even with all the added responsibility I felt more secure, more competent—and certainly much happier—when I was giving directions instead of taking them.

I didn't ponder this revelation, but rather, ate my tunafish (no dressing) and carrot sticks, and then it was time for Iris to change my make-up for the next shot, in which I was wearing a tweed suit, tiger's eye beads and bracelet, and the haughty stare of a New England chatelaine.

The rest of the day was without incident; Holland returned from lunch benignly drunk, and sufficiently aware of his condition to keep his mouth shut. At the end of the afternoon he kissed my cheek as he left and said he probably wouldn't be able to attend the session the next day. I told him I'd miss him, and thanked him for coming. I'm sure everybody else had forgotten the little blip of unpleasantness of that morning; even George, who has been known to hold a grudge or two, waved goodbye to Holland with lighthearted casualness, and Iris kissed the air in his direction.

I couldn't shake the incident, however; it continued to rankle for the rest of the week. I'd never subscribed to the maudlin self-pity of some of my sister models who complained about being mere objects. If they didn't want to be objects at $1000 a day, then let them be typists or sales clerks for less money and more social significance. Yet I suppose some sort of resentment against my career must have been building up for that episode to become such a prominent source of annoyance. For the next few days, everything I did was colored by the memory of Holland's arbitrary and foolish criticism.

I showed nothing, and later in the week, when Holland dropped by the studio, "just to say hi and see how it's going," I greeted him with a convincing little cry of delight, and a peck on the cheek. Rancor, though, foamed in the back of my mind. I was grateful when the assignment ended, even though I knew that one just like it was scheduled in a month. At least during the waiting period I'd have time to myself and would be able to find some sort of photographic work of my own.

Also, I had William's visit to look forward to, even if my anticipation was distorted by an overlay of uneasiness.

Chapter 12

I didn't realize how much I was looking forward to seeing William until the afternoon of the day he was to arrive; I suddenly decided that I would have him over for drinks, maybe even dinner, and that I wanted the apartment to look especially nice. I bought bunches of red-orange roses, tiger lilies and blue thistles at a flower market nearby and placed vases of them in the living room and studio. I shopped for frozen hors d'oeuvres, a thick steak, salad, fruit, cheese, wine, gin and vermouth, a frenzied last-minute foray into the markets and shops on the upper West Side. I realized intermittently that I was acting like some wife of a sea captain expecting her husband home from his world voyage, and I also recognized that I was being extravagantly silly. But then I rationalized my behavior by remembering that it had been a long time since I'd done any entertaining, and, what's more, William was my oldest and most helpful friend. Anyway, I wanted to have him up. That Helen was not accompanying him influenced my decision. With her good manners, her polish, and her ever-present smile, Helen always chilled the evening. It had been years since I'd seen William alone, and I thought we'd feel comfortable and casual together, like the old friends we were.

He was due at Kennedy Airport at seven o'clock, so I knew he wouldn't reach his hotel until at least eight or later, and probably would not call before nine. Around seven I took a long hot bath scented with Chanel, after which I spent at least half an hour doing my face and hair. I put on pink silk lounging pajamas with pants so full they looked like a skirt, and a top cut almost to mid-cleavage. In a fit of childish defiance, I chose my Peretti gold earrings instead of one of the dozens of sets of Bin-Bin Beads that I had on hand. Then I settled back to wait.

The lights were turned down, and Schubert chamber music was on the hi-fi. I was comfortable and confident, and when the phone rang at nine-ten, I let it ring again before answering.

"I'm sorry it's so late," said William, after his greeting. "Is it too late for you? Would you rather put off our meeting until tomorrow morning?"

"Don't be silly," I said. "I'll be furious with you if you don't come by for a drink at least. Have you had dinner?"

"I ate on the plane . . . sort of."

"I have a steak, if you want it."

"Oh, Diane, you shouldn't have. I really thought we'd just meet someplace and I could discuss what I have to discuss. . . ." He hesitated, like someone trying to avoid springing bad news.

"It'll be quieter and pleasanter for you to come by, so go get a cab and get yourself up here."

"Well, OK, if you're sure. . . ."

"I'm sure."

He was there in twenty minutes, wearing a dark suit and tie and carrying a briefcase, like any New York lawyer. I kissed his tanned smooth cheek. There were fine lines around his eyes, and the creases leading from mouth to chin had somewhat deepened, but other than that he had hardly changed. His thick brown hair showed no trace of grey, and his body was still solid and graceful under his establishment suit.

"I thought people who went to California all wore Levis and gold chains," I said, as I led him through the studio to the living room.

He laughed. "Some of us can't escape our past. I sometimes go native out there, but not often."

"Well, take off your jacket and tie and make yourself comfortable," I said lightly, putting my hands on the collar of his jacket. He hesitated, then shrugged out of it. "Give me your tie," I said in a bossy voice. "Otherwise I'll think I'm just entertaining some regular old New Yorker."

He looked uneasy, but did pull his tie loose and hand it to me.

"Good," I said with tour-director jollity. I was beginning to feel a little foolish trying to create an instant intimacy out of what was basically a rather formal situation. "Why don't I mix a couple of drinks and turn on the broiler? If you're hungry, we can fix the steak, and if you're not, well . . . I'll just turn off the broiler."

"I really don't want you to go to any trouble," he protested conventionally.

"Don't be silly," I said, unable to shake my fluttery hostess role. "Make yourself at home, and I'll be right back."

I skipped out to the kitchen and started to mix martinis as I told myself to calm down and stop being so silly. I was trying to impose my idea of my good old friend, William, on the man in the living room. For all I knew they were two different human beings—the reality and my biased memory of him. I was considerably more sedate as I carried in the tray of glasses, shaker and hors d'oevres, and found William still standing almost where I'd left him.

"This is a lovely apartment," he said.

"Yeah. I was lucky to get it." I poured his drink and handed it to him, then poured my own.

We raised our glasses, but did not touch them, and sipped simultaneously. "Well, William," I said, with more restraint, "it's very good to see you. How's Helen?"

"She's fine, and little William's great. They send their love."

After acknowledging and returning the greetings of Helen and his child, I said, "It's a pity you don't get East more often. Or do you like it that way?"

"I like California. But I guess it would be nice to travel a little more. I just wish . . ." he paused and looked at the floor reflectively, then raised his eyes sadly to mine, "I just wish that I had come this time for a different reason."

Completely sobered, I said, "What is it? What's the problem?"

"It's a little awkward, but. . . ."

"William," I laughed mirthlessly. "Don't be so nervous. Come out with it."

He took a deep breath. "First of all, I want you to understand that I'm here on my own. I mean, I'm not a messenger from the firm of Wade and Thomas."

I nodded, watching him.

"I guess they might say—and maybe you, for all I know, will say—that I'm meddling."

"How so?"

"I mean, there might be nothing at all to this. But then again. . . ." He raised his eyebrows over perplexed and sad eyes.

"I don't know what you're talking about, William," I said softly.

"OK. Let me begin at the beginning." He took a sip of the martini and set it on the coffee table. "About a week ago, JoAnn Baxt got in touch with Bin-Bin Beads. Do you know who she is?"

"The gossip columnist?"

"Yeah. She lives here in New York, but she's syndicated all over the country. We read her out in L.A."

"She's mentioned me a couple of times—those 'seen with' types of items. 'Diane Bourne seen with whomever at Studio 54.' I've never met her."

William nodded. "She might mention you again, and it won't be quite so innocuous."

"I can't imagine why."

"She called Mr. Duplessis direct. Fortunately, he was in France, so his secretary took the message. She called to ask if the president of Bin-Bin Beads minded that the Bin-Bin Bead Girl was into dirty pictures. That's exactly how she put it: 'dirty pictures.' " William looked embarrassed.

"She didn't call me," I said, stunned, my stomach falling away from the rest of my body, as though I had been dropped down an elevator shaft.

"No. I found out later why. Since Mr. Duplessis was out of town, the secretary told JoAnn Baxt she wasn't aware of your . . . uh . . . outside activities, and suggested she call the firm's lawyers. Just by luck her call was directed to me." William kept his eyes on the coffee table. "I asked her if she'd checked her story with you, and tried to bluff her about libel, but she's tough. She said there was no need to check with you because she had sworn statements from several of your subjects that you had taken their pictures—and she had the pictures. She was calling Bin-Bin Beads to see whether they knew, and whether this affected their agreement with you."

"She's a bitch," I said coldly.

"She's a gossip columnist," said William philosophically. "She's no worse than most. Anyway, I said we'd have to see the proof that you were involved in that kind of activity before we could make any comment. I thought I'd stall her, and maybe the whole thing would blow over. She said she'd be happy to send prints of the pictures and copies of the statements. She did, and I received them a couple of days ago."

"Is that when you called me?"

"I called you as soon as she'd called. When I talked to you I hadn't seen . . . anything yet."

"I see. Well, this could be interesting." I

looked significantly at his briefcase, which he had put on the floor by his feet.

William looked miserable. "There are some very explicit pictures in some very disreputable magazines, and they're credited to a photographer called D. Bourne. There's no arguing with that."

"No. I certainly wouldn't dispute it."

Still William wouldn't look at me. "I asked Miss Baxt to hold off investigating further—that is, talking to Mr. Duplessis—until I'd talked to you. He's still out of the country, anyway, so that wasn't too difficult to arrange. But she won't be put off much longer—the story's too good, and she's afraid someone else will scoop her. I should call her tomorrow, in fact. And also talk to the other members of my firm and to Wade and Thomas. And maybe get in touch with Mr. Duplessis in France."

"This seems like an awful lot of fuss over nothing."

William's head snapped up and his eyes widened in either surprise or anger. "For Christ's sake, Diane, don't you have any sense of responsibility? Don't you know what a story like this could do to you? And to Bin-Bin Beads?"

I was stunned by his vehemence. Coldly, I said, "To be frank, William, it's no one's business what I do on my own time."

He stared at me disbelievingly. "You don't have your own time. You don't have—can't have—a private life. I told you when the job first came up that next to appearance, the most important thing for the Bin-Bin Bead Girl to be was above reproach. That means twenty-four hours a day. You're a symbol for the company, and you're wholesome, fun-loving and girl-next-door. You are *not* the kind of girl who takes dirty pictures."

Chastised, I said nothing.

William, as though he regretted his harshness, added more softly, "Even those other pictures—the ones for fashion magazines—weren't exactly what the Bin-Bin Bead Girl should be messing around with."

"The Bin-Bin Bead Girl doesn't have a camera, in other words," I said, with what I hoped was an unreadable expression.

He gestured impatiently. "You know that's not what I'm saying, Diane. It's just that as long as you're under contract to Bin-Bin Beads, you should devote all your time to them. Theoretically. If you want to take pictures, fine. But don't go around getting them published. You're a full-time representative for the firm. You shouldn't have time to work two jobs. Or three." He looked at me questioningly. "I assume you separate the pictures you do for *Fashion* from those that appeared in . . . *Horny Nights*."

"Not particularly," I said calmly. "Each publication presented its own problems, which I solved. I'm a very good photographer, and plan to get better." I looked levelly at him.

He leaned forward on the couch, his elbows on his knees, his head drooping as he studied the floor. With a sigh he said, almost to himself, "I came here thinking that I'd find out that you and D. Bourne were two different people. I knew that wasn't likely, but still I hoped it would happen—that you'd be shocked and angry and we'd discover some flesh and blood D. Bourne who was into dirty pictures. There's no chance denying that D. Bourne and you are the same person."

"I wouldn't do that," I said. "I'm not ashamed of any of those pictures. They're good work."

Exasperated, he stood up. "But don't you see, Diane, that most people are going to see these pictures and think that not only do you take them, you also do the things you're photographing. It's guilt by association, in a sense, and it's not fair, but there it is. Your private life is going to be besmirched if all this comes to light." He paused and lowered his voice. "In fact, one of the men you photographed swears that you did join in an orgy. JoAnn Baxt sent me a copy of his statement."

"Who was that?" I asked.

William snapped open his briefcase and shuffled through some manilla envelopes. From one of them he withdrew a paper and looked at it. "Vince Carleton," he said.

I blushed. Though I kept my expression blank, I could not stop the flow of red suffusing my face. "That asshole," I said.

Looking more embarrassed than ever, William said, "Is it true? Can he prove it?"

"Yes. There were witnesses."

William shook his head and sat down again. "How in God's name could you do this, Diane? I mean, even if you didn't have a professional commitment, an image to maintain, how could you do something like this? You aren't that kind of girl."

Something snapped, and I turned on William so

furiously he recoiled. "You pompous jerk. What do you mean I'm not that kind of girl? *What* kind of girl? How dare you sit there wrapped in smugness and judge me! For the first time since I can remember I'm comfortable with myself—more than that: I'm *proud* of myself. And you come here and whine because I happen to have fucked a couple of guys—or more. So what?"

Trying to restore calm, to himself as well as to me, William lowered his voice and spoke with that reasonableness that lawyers frequently mistake for logic. "I'm not here to judge your sex life, Diane. That's of no concern to me—to us. What I am here to try to rectify is the publicity that might stem from your . . . affairs."

"They weren't affairs," I said defiantly. "At least, most of them weren't. They were one-night stands. And there've been a lot of them." It was true, but hardly necessary to tell William. I was trying to shock him out of his role as lawyer and into a more human position as my friend. I wanted him to know everything; I wanted his approval.

His confusion was apparent, and I guessed that it was a personal as well as a professional response. He didn't know how to take this information. "There's no need to go into all that," he said. "All I have to do—all we have to do—is figure out some way to keep this information from the papers. Specifically from JoAnn Baxt."

"Is JoAnn Baxt going to print that I've fucked a few men? Let her. I don't care." Sullenly, I curled up at the other end of the sofa, my arms crossed on my chest.

William looked at me with what seemed genuine distress. "You really have changed. You're so different from when I met you. I feel responsible in a way. I got you involved in this."

"Just what kind of fairy tale have you created around me, William?"

Surprised, he watched me from his corner of the sofa with a pained expression.

"What do you think you got me involved in?" I continued calmly and superciliously. "I'm a very normal woman indulging, as far as I'm concerned, in very normal tastes. Perhaps I have a few more occasions than most women to satisfy myself sexually, but I don't think I could hold a candle to most men. You, for example, have probably gone in for more hanky-panky than I have, and thought nothing of it. Because you're a man."

He was stung into a blush of his own. "I've never once been unfaithful to Helen," he said quickly.

This enraged me. At the time I thought it was because of the prissiness of his admission, but later I recognized that my reaction was shot through with veins of jealousy. "If that's a boast," I said, "it's pathetic. Are you so cowed that in all these years you haven't dared stray a little?"

"I'm not cowed. We love each other, and are satisfied with our marriage and our child."

"Do you mean you haven't once even wanted to play around? I don't believe you."

"If I ever did, I would quell the impulse," he said, so defensively he surprised me.

"You're stacking up an awful lot of regrets for

your golden years, then," I said sarcastically, delighted to have him against a wall.

He was still flushed, and his eyes were bright with anger. I reflected how ironic it was for me to be ridiculing him for his chastity. Stiffly, he said, "I think we've gotten off the subject. I didn't fly here to discuss my sexual habits, or yours, for that matter. I'm here to see what we can do about stanching some potentially harmful, even devastating, gossip. As I said, I'd hoped you might deny that you'd ever taken the pictures that JoAnn Baxt says you did. Now I see that's out of the question. So we have to figure some way to keep the facts from going public."

I was still tingling from my brush against William's admission that not once had he been unfaithful to Helen. It continued to sting me like a grasped nettle. "I have no intention of lying," I said.

"I'm not asking you to lie. That's the last thing I'd do." He looked at me reproachfully, his legal integrity challenged. "What we've got to do is find some way to negotiate with the woman and convince her to desist."

"If she doesn't print it, someone else will," I said. "After all, it's hardly a secret. I've used my own name, and done a lot of work. And if Vince Carleton has a hair up his ass, he'll see to it that some other columnist gets the word."

"Why is he so vindictive?"

I shrugged. "I didn't want to see him again. I guess that's why. Who knows? Maybe he's just an asshole, as I said. But I did turn him down."

"You mean, you didn't sleep with him?" asked William.

"No, that's not what I mean. I mean I didn't sleep with him twice."

"Oh."

"Look. Let her run the item. Diane Bourne takes dirty pictures. So what? If she wants to go further and say Diane Bourne fucks men—and maybe a few women—who's going to care for very long?"

"Women? You've had affairs with women?"

"Not affairs."

"But relations with women?"

"A couple."

William gazed hopelessly at the coffee table. Our drinks were only half finished and had turned warm. The hors d'oeuvres were cold and greasy. It even seemed, though this was surely an illusion, that all the flowers I'd so carefully placed around the room were somewhat wilted.

"For heaven's sake, William, it isn't the end of the world. It's not going to bother me that much if this stuff appears in the papers."

"It may not bother you," he flared, "but it'll play hell with Bin-Bin Beads. Damnit, Diane, you're not a baby. Bin-Bin has given you one of the most expensive contracts ever written to represent them. They've paid for your image. If this gets out, that image will be tarnished—probably irrevocably. Who's going to look at beads in those commercials when the word gets out that the girl wearing them. . . ." He stopped, embarrassed.

". . . fucks everything in sight," I finished for him. "I'm sorry, William. You're right. I am being irresponsible. I can't bring myself to apologize for what I've done—for my photographs—because the work meant, and still means, a lot to me. But I've been foolish this evening." I moved closer and put my hand on his shoulder. "Let's start the evening over. Maybe we can find some way to get around this thing." I was genuinely contrite, for I realized that not only was the impending gossip item a crisis for me, it was also serious for William, who had vouched for me. I hated hurting someone who had tried so hard to help me. "Let me mix a fresh drink—these are warm. OK?"

He looked relieved, as though I'd come to my senses, and perhaps I had. "Sure, that'd be fine." He patted my hand, which still rested on his shoulder.

"How about that steak?" I asked as I gathered our glasses and the shaker.

"I don't think I could eat anything right now," he said.

I nodded and took the paraphernalia for mixing martinis to the kitchen, along with the now unappetizing appetizers. I was gone only a few minutes. When I returned he was leaning back against the sofa, his eyes closed. I studied him briefly. The strain of our meeting told on his face; there was a tenseness around the lips, as though he were clenching his teeth, and his eyes were squeezed shut. They opened when I put the tray on the table near his briefcase. I sat near him and poured two drinks.

"OK," I said gently. "What is it we've got to deal with?" I looked at his briefcase.

He sat up, sighed, and pulled the briefcase toward him. From it he took a stack of magazines and selected *Honey*, which fell open to the centerfold. There was the black, highlighted ass that had been my first venture into skin publications. Wordlessly William pointed to the credit, in tiny letters: "Photograph by D. Bourne." He shook his head.

"Why didn't you at least take another name?" he asked.

"Good question. At the time it just never occurred to me. I suppose that sounds naive, but it's true. Anyway I was proud of the work. I would even have been willing to use Diane Bourne, but the editor wouldn't allow it. We compromised on D. Bourne, so people couldn't guess my gender." I looked at the picture of the gleaming ass. "Then, too, I was still just a model, and not yet the Bin-Bin Bead Girl. Though I don't think that would have mattered to me much. I probably still would have kept my own name. At least before now." I smiled ruefully. "Now, of course, I'd change it to Joe Smith, since I've learned how much trouble it's causing."

Reproachfully, William said, "You've never been 'just a model,' Diane. You've been well known, right from the beginning."

"I've been luckier than most, but hardly well known. You know what I mean. Most people don't attach names to models . . . only those in the business. And people in the trade are a fairly sophisticated bunch, and they're not going to care if I shoot a few dirty pictures. Or fuck a few men."

William winced, but refrained from criticizing my language. Instead, he said, "People in the trade are going to start caring if the general public gets wind of what you've been up to. This could wreck your career, Diane."

"Oh, William, come on. In this day and age? Do you really think people are going to be so outraged? I'm not doing anything half the country isn't doing—or wants to."

Solemnly William turned to me. "Half the country is not beamed out of TV sets and plastered on billboards and exposed in glossy magazines. Half the country isn't a symbol. You are a symbol, you're well paid to be a symbol. And people expect more from symbols than they expect from their friends, their acquaintances and, above all, from themselves. A model in your position becomes a kind of idol—maybe it's a leftover from paganism, I don't know, but you are looked up to. You're a sort of goddess. And goddesses don't take dirty pictures and sleep around in such a manner so as to get caught at it. You can do whatever you want, so long as you don't do it publicly. Publicly, you don't . . . fuck around." He almost strangled on the word, and after saying it had to clear his throat. "Surely Harold Ames must have warned you? If he didn't he's been remiss as your agent."

"Harold doesn't know about the skin mags. Why should he? He's not the sort of guy to read them, and there hasn't been any gossip. He did know about the fashion photography, but I don't think he took it very seriously. He saw it more as a hobby than anything else." I thought for a minute and added, "If he had ever come down hard on me about my photography, I would have changed agencies. I'm hot enough now to be able to write my own ticket, and I don't have to put up with that kind of hassle from an agency."

William thought that over, then clicked his tongue once in punctuation to his distress. He took another magazine from the pile, *Hot Man.* On the cover was a muscular man astride a motorcycle, his bulging arms akimbo, and his blue-denimed crotch inflated with what promised to be an epic hard-on. He glared directly at the camera with defiant, smoldering eyes which were planted midway between bristling black mustache and cropped black hair. "Eric takes it all off!!!" was the tag line printed across his thigh. William turned to the centerfold and there was the same man, legs spread, cock erect, balls billowing, pecs swelling, eyes inviting. "Photographs by D. Bourne" was barely noticeable in the lower left corner.

We both looked at the picture wordlessly for a few minutes, then William said accusingly, "This is a homosexual publication."

"That's right. They don't pay much."

"For our present purposes, that isn't their only drawback. It's bad enough to go in for this sort of thing—the pictures, I mean—but to do it for perverts just makes it that much worse, if the word gets out."

By this time I had stopped trying to refute William, even in my own head. I resignedly accepted his judgment, putting the solution to the problem in his hands. He flipped through several more magazines: *Docks, Meat, Breathless, Hot Lips, Horny Nights.* Wordlessly he pointed to each of my contributions with their identifying signature: D. Bourne.

As he opened to the orgy scene in *Horny Nights* he looked grimmer.

In a neutral voice I said, "That's Vince Carleton," as I pointed him out.

William studied the picture. "He's the one you . . . ah . . ."

"One of them. Actually I had sex with all of them." I was no longer defiant, but rather, confiding, as thought I were detailing symptoms for a sympathetic family doctor.

"The woman, too?" asked William.

"No. She came before we could get anything going with each other. Just the men."

"Where was this?"

"In my studio. The other studio—the one downtown. Not many people know about it."

"I see." He continued to look at the pictures, and I realized that his interest in this layout—and probably the others as well—was more than legal. Poor William was breathing a little more rapidly than when he'd arrived.

The discovery ignited a corresponding fuse in me. Until that moment, I'd overlooked the suppressed fantasies I might have felt about William, and had transposed him into the role of confessor, duenna and disciplinarian. In short, he had become an authority figure who'd materialized to tell me what a naughty girl I'd been. When I saw his face flushed, his mouth open, and his eyes fixed on my photographs, all his social armor dissolved, and he became vulnerably human for me. With swelling tenderness I put my hand on his shoulder and said, "The pictures are pretty good, aren't they?"

William flinched as though I'd slipped an ice cube down his back. He was shocked, not at my gesture but at his own susceptibility. He turned toward me as though he were inserting an invisible wedge between us, and stiffly said, "I really don't know. I don't know that much about photography. They are very clear and detailed, certainly."

I was touched, rather than put off by his reaction. I laughed gently, encouragingly, and said, "I wasn't talking about the pictures as pictures, but about the content. They're very erotic—I mean they do arouse, don't they?"

"I suppose they would if you went in for that sort of thing."

I laughed teasingly. "Oh, come off it, William. I caught you staring. Don't be so stuffy."

He dropped a swatch of dignity over his face. "I suppose I must seem stuffy to you. The fact is, though, that I really don't care for pornography." He raised his hand to forestall any comment and hastily added, "I absolutely approve of anyone's right to publish and read it, don't get me wrong. I'm one hundred per cent against censorship. But I myself have never understood its function."

"Haven't you ever felt that possibly there were other ways to make love than those you indulge in?"

"I haven't given the matter that much thought."

"I find that hard to believe, William."

He shrugged.

"Surely, you've had fantasies, daydreams, thought up combinations and games and couplings. . . ."

"I told you, Diane, I've never been unfaithful to Helen."

"Well Helen must be quite a girl to keep you so in harness."

I could see him debate whether or not to take umbrage. He chose to be ultra-reasonable. "Helen and I enjoy a very satisfactory intimacy."

"But," I persisted, "haven't you ever seen someone on the street, some passing form, that enticed you, set your imagination to ranging?"

Exasperated, he said, "What I think and what I do are two different things." Immediately he regretted his words.

"So you *do* let your mind wander now and then," I said, laughing, wagging my finger under his nose. I felt playfully in control, as though I were winning a little game. I moved closer and took his face between my hands. "I wonder what you're thinking now."

He remained absolutely still for a few seconds, without even blinking his eyes. Then, with a deep breath, as though he were just waking up, he pulled his head from my hands and looked away. I felt him tense to rise, but he stayed seated. In that instant he made a decision. I leaned over and kissed him on the lips.

For the briefest moment he was passive, then a shadow of withdrawal coursed through his body; then he put his arms around me and returned my kiss. I flowed into his arms, pressing my breast against his, and opening my mouth so that our tongues could find each other. We kissed, each exploring every contour of the other's lips, as William held me tightly around my waist. I leaned my head against his shoulder, reveling in the accelerated heaving of our chests.

William said, "This is not fair to any of us."

I put my hand over his lips. "Don't. Don't start thinking beyond right now."

He paused before saying, "I can't ignore my responsibility to . . ."

Again I shut him up. "William, this is a very simple situation. We're going to do something that is going to make us feel good, that will hurt no one, and that will have absolutely no consequences."

"Everything has consequences."

"Only if you allow them. Or, more to the point, only if you encourage them."

His hands, spread wide, traveled up my back, crumpling the pink silk against my flesh, pressing so hard he outlined my ribs. I touched his face, then smoothed his hair back from his forehead. His eyes gleamed thoughtful and intense out of his flushed face. "I have to be honest, Diane. Whatever we do, I can't promise more. I have a family, and I can't, I won't. . . ."

I laughed. "Oh, William. Are you saying you won't make an honest woman out of me?"

He continued to stare at me, unamused. "I just don't want any misunderstandings. . . ."

"Your problem is that you're too damned conscientious. There is no misunderstanding. It's a very clear proposition. All I'm going to do is fuck you and send you back to Helen. How's that for clarity?"

His eyes widened in surprise, but otherwise his

expression remained solemn. I put my hands on his cheeks and kissed him deeply, and after a second he responded. Drawing back I said, "Let's go to the bedroom," and got to my feet while holding on to his hand. He stood and followed docilely as I led him through the door and to the edge of the bed.

I turned toward him, unbuttoned his shirt and pulled it out of his pants, then put my arms around his naked torso. The hair of his chest was feather soft. I opened my blouse, and we swayed slightly against each other, with only a hint of contact. He lowered my blouse off the shoulders, and it slid to the floor as I unsnapped his cuff links and pulled his shirt down his arms. With his lips on mine, he unsnapped my bra, then stooped to kiss the hollow of my throat as I caressed his head.

He straightened, and we faced each other; the brown curling hair on his pectorals barely brushed my nipples as we looked into each other's eyes. William was somber, almost grim, breathing through a half-open mouth.

Smiling encouragement, I unbuckled his belt and opened his fly. His trousers slid down his legs, exposing white jockey shorts, the same type he had worn sixteen years before in a Yale dormitory. I traced the bulge of his cock with my palm, then knelt and held my open mouth close to but not on it. He entwined my hair around his fingers and whimpered. I guided him around so that his back was to the bed, then I gently pushed him down on it. He sat as I removed his shoes and socks and pulled down his trousers. Then I stood and stepped out of my pants and panties.

"My God, you're beautiful," he whispered.

William ceased to be passive. Until then he had permitted himself to be led from one stage of seduction to the next, as though his desire were some malleable substance that I could shape into any form I wished. When I stood naked before him, he rose and drew me to him, taking command of me. He kissed my neck, breasts, ears, eyes, lips—token brushes with his puckered mouth, like a predator staking out his territory. I thrilled at each touch, and my legs became weaker as he grew more forceful. He pulled down his underwear, his cock emerging from his pubic hair, hard and red-tipped. I stepped close to him so that his cock slid between my thighs, and put my arms around his waist. With one of his hands on my ass, and the other on my back, he lifted me and lowered me to the bed, then knelt over me. He swooped to my breast and took a nipple in his mouth, and at the same time held my head on the pillow with both hands. As his body pressed against mine, I was immobilized, captured by his weight.

He moved to my other breast. I took his head in my hands, but he pinned down my arms so that they were aligned with my body, and I was unable to use them. His cock rubbed against my legs as he sucked one nipple, then the other. After a few minutes, during which I moaned and squirmed, he took my hands in his and licked his way down to my navel, where he paused long enough to circle it with his tongue. Then, going lower, he inserted his tongue into my pussy and touched my clitoris. The convulsive shudder of my orgasm surprised both of us.

William looked at me questioningly, as though asking whether he should continue, and I reached down to pull his head up to mine so our lips could meet. I held him tightly, then turned, forcing him to lie on his side so that we faced each other. I pushed him onto his back, then began a downward path along his torso that was similar to the route he had followed along mine. I sucked his nipples, then tongued the hard ridge down to his navel, and lower, to his cock. I passed over the cock and took his balls in my mouth—one at a time at first, then both, as I rubbed my hands over his taut, hairy abdomen. I took his balls in my hand and licked the shaft of his cock, working from the base toward the head. His back arched in anticipation as I got nearer the tip and circled it without touching it. Spasms ran through his cock, causing it to throb in time with his heartbeat. I poised over the red glistening head for an instant, then took it in my mouth, bathing it with circular swipes of my tongue. He gasped and bucked as his body grew rigid, and for a moment I thought he had come. But there was no salty taste, and when I took my mouth away, his cock was still hard and pulsing. William grabbed me by the shoulders and pulled me up the length of his body; I felt his cock, wet with my saliva, flatten and slide between my breasts, over my belly, and across the slit of my pussy. We kissed long and deeply, making little groans of pleasure as our hands explored nipples, ass, waist, cock and pussy.

Suddenly, William turned and, holding me

tightly, reversed our positions, so that I was flattened once more under his weight. As he pressed his mouth against mine, he undulated his hips so that his cock slid back and forth across my pussy, causing me to spread my legs and lift my hips in an effort to lure him inside me. His kisses became more violent, almost painful as he sucked at my lips and ears and throat in an effort, it seemed, to consume me. My arms were flung around his back and my legs were stretched down the length of his, with my feet meeting over his calves, pressing my pussy to his cock, which, hard and demanding, still had not entered me. We remained locked, as though in combat, each trying to overwhelm the other.

William broke our clasp by raising his buttocks over my thighs. He floated above me for a second, then descended as his cock entered my pussy, guided only by our mutual need. Slowly he penetrated, coaxing me into openness, invading my depths. I was so attuned to him that I could feel, or thought I could, the veins of his cock as it filled my pussy. When our pubic hair met, and it seemed he could go no farther, he pressed harder as though to conquer every inner niche of my being. He remained still for a moment, as we both savored the sensation of our union, then slowly he began to pump up and down, rotating his cock spasmodically in a quest to heighten his own pleasure, and mine.

Several times he almost withdrew, bringing the head of his cock right to the edge of the inner lips of my pussy; he would hesitate there, quivering, then plunge again. Our open mouths held our heads together as each tongue darted into the other's dark wet sanctuary. My hands moved over William's back in a frantic effort to pull us even closer, and my legs wrapped around his hips to keep him captive inside me.

William thrust again and again, and I felt the onslaught of my next orgasm racing through my nerves, rushing to my pussy, and suddenly I screamed as pleasure exploded in my thighs.

My cry spurred William to quicken his tempo. He bounced on me ever more rapidly and lifted his lips from mine as he began to moan. I held him as tightly as I could, but his passion furnished escape from my grasp as with a great groan he tensed, and his pelvis jerked as semen flowed from his cock. I could feel the spurt of liquid, like white lava, flooding my pussy.

With a shudder he collapsed and buried his face in my neck. I clasped his head and rubbed my cheek against his as he lay on top of me.

"Am I too heavy?" he whispered, not moving.

"No. You're just right."

He shifted, as though to retrieve his cock.

"Don't," I said, my hands on his ass. "Leave it there."

Sighing, he settled on me as our breathing became regular and steady, then deeper, and we drifted off to sleep.

I was wakened—I wasn't sure how much later—as William, still lying on and in me, gently kissed my face, eyes and ears. I opened my eyes to stare directly into his, which were only inches away, regarding me somberly, almost sadly.

"Did you have a good sleep?" he asked.

"Yes." I squeezed him with my arms. "You?"

"Yes." He rubbed his nose against mine and stroked my hair. He raised himself on his elbows and looked at me for a long moment, then gently retrieved his cock and moved from on top of me to my side. The air that touched my body—now moist with our mingled sweat—was cold, like the air from a newly opened ancient cave. I shivered.

"What's wrong?" he asked, his hand rubbing my breasts and belly.

In answer I turned to him and snuggled closer, my arms around his neck. He rubbed my back and ass for a moment, then sighed.

"I guess . . ." he stopped.

"You guess you'd better be going," I said into his chest.

He was still a moment. "I don't want to."

"Then don't."

"But I have to call . . . home."

"You can call from here."

He was silent again. Then, "No, I can't. This is why I didn't want this to happen. Deceit isn't something I handle well."

"Then you must not be a very good lawyer."

"That's not funny, Diane." But he smiled, then grew serious again. "I mean personal deceit. I mean. . . ."

"You mean you don't like to lie to Helen. Especially if I'm around to hear it."

His silence was agreement.

I pulled back from him and rested my head on my hand. We lay, propped on our elbows, facing each other, like figures on an Etruscan vase. "Are you hungry?" I asked.

He looked thoughtful. "I am," he said, in some surprise.

"I'll fix the steak. The broiler's still on. That is, if the kitchen hasn't gone up in flames by this time."

"Are you sure you want to go to all that trouble?" he asked, with a polite formality that sat strangely on our naked bodies.

"Quite sure. I'm starved myself." I rolled out of bed and stood looking down at him. Quickly I bent and kissed him before going to the bathroom.

When I came out William was sitting on the edge of the bed, in his underwear and socks, his elbows on his knees, looking at the floor. As I approached he glanced up with an expression so confused and woebegone that I laughed.

"Did you lose your shoes?" I asked.

"Worse. I think I lost my mind." He shook his head. "Diane, I'm so sorry about this. . . ."

"William," I said, exasperated, commanding him to silence. "I hope you aren't going to wallow in remorse. If nothing else, it's rude."

He looked stricken. "I didn't mean to imply that I regretted making love to you, it's just that I wish things were different . . . I don't know how, really. I'm sorry, I'm not good at adultery."

"Practice, then." I kissed him.

He shook his head again, a rueful smile on his lips. "You've changed so much."

"That happens to the best of us. And a good thing too."

"But what's going to become of you . . . of us?"

"I'll be very surprised if anything becomes of us." I laughed. "Anyway, that's supposed to be my line. This whole discussion is backwards, do you realize that? Here I am, the seduced maiden, comforting and reassuring my seducer."

"I'd say the seduction was pretty well balanced between us," said William drily.

"You'd be right." I knelt on the bed and put my arms around his neck. "Come on, don't be so morose. You don't have any scars, and you haven't left any."

He smiled at me and returned my kiss. "God, it was wonderful, Diane."

"For me too," I said sincerely. We held each other a moment longer, satiated, comfortable, loving. "I'm not used to fucking old friends. It's a good feeling."

He stiffened in disapproval, but said nothing. Teasingly, I kissed him again. "Do you want your steak in bed or at the table?"

"At the table, I think," he said primly.

After kissing him again, I put on my robe and went to the kitchen.

By the time the steak was broiled, the salad made and the wine opened, William was dressed and sitting on the sofa near his open briefcase. The magazines were still spread where we had left them before going to the bedroom, and the questions they had raised remained unanswered. Neither of us mentioned the reason for William's visit as we sat down to the candlelit table. The flowers I had lavished on the apartment once again looked fresh and opulent as the flicker of the flames danced over them. We ate rapidly, mostly silently, like a couple accustomed to meals together; we were both ravenous. As I cleared away the plates and brought in a bowl of fruit, William kissed my palm, pressing it to his lips. I smoothed his hair with my other hand, and leaned against him.

Sadly, he looked up at me. "I've got to do something about those photographs tomorrow."

"It doesn't look like there's much to be done. They exist. I took them. JoAnn Baxt needs a story."

"Maybe there's something I can do to keep the story out of the papers and away from Mr. Duplessis. I'll talk to Miss Baxt tomorrow." He didn't sound very hopeful.

"Don't do anything to risk your own position," I said. "I mean, don't try to cover up for me, if it'll mean catching your ass in a crack."

William smiled. "My ass will be in a tighter crack if the news gets out than if it doesn't. It's my job to keep everyone—not from knowing—but from having to acknowledge that the Bin-Bin Bead Girl takes dirty pictures."

"What can you do?"

"I can plead with JoAnn Baxt." Distaste was in his voice and expression.

"I'm sorry, William."

He pulled me down on his lap. "I see now you couldn't really have known. You were foolish, God knows, but I guess you were too involved in getting work with a camera to understand the consequences.

Does being a photographer really mean so much to you?"

"Yes. It's more important than anything else in my life."

"Even more important than being a top model?"

"Of course."

"And what about . . . you know, personal relationships. Surely you'll want to settle down, have a family. . . ."

I laughed. "William, at this moment that's the least of my concerns. I have a career to create. Once I feel secure in it, then I'll see."

He shook his head thoughtfully. "I'm not very up to date."

I kissed him. "You're simply perfect the way you are: loyal, helpful, kind—and a marvelous fuck."

"Please don't, Diane," he said seriously. "I can't get used to your talking that way. It's as though you had become hard—and I know you haven't."

Tenderly, I leaned against his shoulder. "It's a veneer, a sort of protection, for me to assume. I guess it's an attitude, and a helpful one for a girl to have. I can't give it up, but I can promise not to put it on when you're around."

He was silent. Then, hesitantly, "I'm not going to be around very much, you know."

"I know. But *if* you are, *when* you are, you'll find the same sweet little Diane you first knew sixteen years ago."

We both laughed, and he said, "I don't think I'd settle for that either."

"I know good and well you wouldn't. Neither would I."

We moved back to the living room where William gathered up the copies of *Docks, Meat, Honey* and so on, and put them into his staid briefcase as though he were scooping a load of hookers into a convent. He snapped the catch; its decisive ring echoed through the apartment like a slammed door. That sound declared the evening finished.

With our arms around each other we walked through the studio to the entrance, and I paused to kiss him again, molding myself to his body.

"Good-bye, Diane."

"Good night."

At the elevator he turned to wave. I stood at the door, smiling until the elevator came. I was still smiling as I shut my door, though there were tears coursing down my cheeks.

Epilogue

There was, of course, no question of JoAnn Baxt passing up a good story. For her it was one day's sensation; for me it was the end of a career. Yet I didn't hold it against her. I think, really, that if I were entirely honest, I was rather relieved, for after the flurry and fuss and the demands for interviews, and the denials issued by Wade and Thomas—after all the dust had settled, I found myself curiously relaxed.

"Bin-Bin Bead Girl go Bang-Bang?" ran the headline in *Variety,* and the story proceeded to say that Diane Bourne, according to columnist JoAnn Baxt, had been taking dirty pictures (and probably doing more than that) for the last few years. There was a lot of innuendo. After the initial shock I became indifferent, as though the debacle were happening to someone else. My only regret was that people around me were hurt. Harold Ames and Anita both were as loyal as one would expect them to be to their highest paid model, but beyond that they were sincerely concerned about me. William, out on the coast, took a lot of flack for having introduced me and vouched for me. He didn't lose his position—he was a partner in his firm, after all—but he did lose, at least for a while, a certain standing, and he was embarrassed. The only lucky thing to happen during the whole mess was that not once was his name linked to mine in any of the stories printed.

The scandal was put into perspective for me by Mr. Mane, whom I met one afternoon on Fifth Avenue. He saw me first and waved with his old-fashioned courtesy, and asked, "How's your work going?"

He was referring to my photography, I knew, without his having to specify. "Not very well at the moment," I said dolefully. "You know, there's been some bad publicity lately, and. . . ."

"Oh?" he said, surprised. Then his face cleared as he recalled, "Oh, yes, that bead thing, your photographs for the girlie magazines."

I smiled at the phrase "girlie magazines." And nodded.

"Well," he said indifferently, "I wouldn't worry about that. That'll blow over. You know, I did some nudes about . . . oh, it must have been about forty years ago. They were considered very risqué then. They look like art now." He patted my hand. "Of course, I wasn't as pretty as you, so no one paid as much attention to me as they do to you. The important thing is to keep working, isn't it?"

"Yes," I said, knowing it was the truth.

But it was as difficult for me to keep working in photography as it was to model. My notoriety, briefly, was so great that I was more of a walking news item than a model or photographer. The fashion magazines wouldn't touch me, and the department stores and catalog people were equally uninterested. For a while, as far as the fashion world was concerned, I was in limbo.

There remained the skin mags. They certainly didn't mind the publicity, but by this time I was wary of becoming further associated with any of them, particularly since several reporters had found out the address of my downtown studio and staked a watch out to see who I showed up with. I couldn't risk any more coverage of that sort.

Bin-Bin Beads did not fire me. They couldn't, really, since I had a contract with them. What they did, however, was comparable to declaring me a non-person: I simply disappeared. One day I was swirling through television spots, beaming from glossy magazines, dominating throughways from billboards, and the next day all trace of me was obliterated. What's more, Bin-Bin Beads decided to take, as the business pages called it, a low profile for several months until the adverse publicity dissipated. After that time, according to a spokesman for the firm, Bin-Bin would re-evaluate its promotional campaign. I had wanted more free time. I certainly got it.

For the first couple of weeks, I stayed close to my apartment, because I didn't want to risk being recognized and hounded. Then, in dark glasses and with a scarf on my head, I started walking around the city with my Nikon, like a tourist. It was not as satisfying as working on an assignment, but it was better than brooding alone.

Harold Ames could have gotten me a couple of "parts" jobs. My hands or eyes or legs were all extremely photogenic, but I couldn't accept them without violating my contract with Bin-Bin Beads, which called for my exclusive services, even if they didn't want them. Harold asked if I wanted him to get me out of the contract so I could go back to work. It would have meant losing the large sum that Bin-Bin had committed to me, but on the other hand I would have been able, theoretically, to begin to rebuild my modeling career.

I said no. I realized that I wanted the time this scandal had inadvertently given me. I wanted to discover the person I'd become over the last four years, during which my life had changed so dramatically. I didn't even want to leave the city, but rather I preferred to remain where the change had taken place. I found that, as I had told William the night he came to see me, I really did like the person I had become. My experience as a model had diluted my chronic insecurity, though it would probably always be with me to some degree, and my work as a photographer granted me a purpose I never had before. I was pleased, and at the same time impatient for the nonsensical scandal to blow over so I could get on with this life I found so worth living.

It took time. After a couple of months I began to ease back into making the rounds to art directors and editors, showing them my work, pushing for jobs. Notoriety, like fame, is fleeting. Most people in the business looked vague when they saw me, as though they were searching some file cabinet in their brain for a misplaced item. Then their faces would relax as they remembered, oh, yes, there'd been something about some naughty photos, caused a flap for a while, she's the Bin-Bin Bead Girl—or was, or something. . . .

Harold Ames kept urging me to resume modeling as soon as the contract with Bin-Bin ran out, and I kept putting him off. Then, one day, I said, "I'm going to call it quits, Harold. I'm too old for the business."

"That's ridiculous. You're thirty, and you've never looked better. You could work another thirty years. That's the advantage of being a products model, and not in fashion."

"But I don't want the hassle. I've got other things to do." I spoke with finality.

Sadly he stared to the right of my face. During our four years together he had never once looked directly into my eyes. I put my hand on his arm. "Thank you for everything, Harold. I could never have done so well without you."

My good-bye to Anita—even though it was hardly final, and we would be seeing each other from time to time—was tearful. We both sobbed and cried; but I left the agency feeling as though I'd just graduated from a particularly harsh school.

I landed a job shooting a layout of fall skirts and sweaters for *Fashion.* I set up in a private S and M club and got the most innocent and sweetest-looking models I could find. The contrast of their wide-eyed, scrubbed faces with chains hanging from the ceiling and black leather-clad attendants of both sexes caused a lot of talk and brought me new business. Before too long I was on my way as a full-time photographer, building a reputation for kinky but quality work. I let my downtown studio go.

Ever since he had left New York the last time, William called at least once a week—concerned, worried calls which were confined to asking me how I was weathering the storm. Never did he mention our evening together, nor did I. He always sent Helen's best wishes, and a couple of times, when he called from home, she got on the phone to convey—in her carefully modulated, well-bred voice—her hopes that everything was working out all right. I always assured both of them that I was just dandy.

Then, yesterday, William called in the early afternoon, my time.

"Listen," he said after we had asked each other how we were feeling, "I've got to go to New York tomorrow."

"Great," I said calmly.

"Yeah. There's some trouble with one of our clients."

"Is Helen coming with you?" I asked politely.

"No. She can't make it. She's tied up out here, and anyway it'll only be for a couple of days."

"Why don't you plan to have dinner here when you get in, then," I asked, my voice casual and as neutral as his.

"Oh, I don't want to put you to any trouble . . ."

"No trouble. I'll get a steak, or something easy, if that's OK."

"Well, if you're sure you don't mind."

"Not at all. It'll be nice seeing you."

"I'll get there about eight-thirty. Shall I come straight to your apartment from the airport?"

"Why don't you? I'll see you then. Oh, and tell Helen hi for me."

"Will do." He hung up.

So now I have to go and buy some flowers and wine and maybe some scented candles. I think this may be the beginning of a bi-coastal affair.

I'm fairly certain I can handle it.